LOCOMOTIVE
BUILDING

THE CONSTRUCTION OF A STEAM ENGINE FOR RAILWAY USE

BY RALPH E. FLANDERS

THE CLASSIC
STEAM LOCOMOTIVE BOOK
FROM 1911

MACHINERY'S REFERENCE SERIES

EACH NUMBER IS ONE UNIT IN A COMPLETE LIBRARY OF MACHINE DESIGN AND SHOP PRACTICE REVISED AND REPUBLISHED FROM MACHINERY

NUMBER 79

LOCOMOTIVE BUILDING

By Ralph E. Flanders

PART I

MAIN AND SIDE RODS

CONTENTS

LOCOMOTIVE BUILDING

MAIN AND SIDE RODS

Altoona is the focus of railway activity in western Pennsylvania. It forms the terminal of the Eastern and Western Pennsylvania Divisions, and there is scarcely a moment of the day when trains are not arriving or departing. The density of the traffic is best realized, perhaps, by sitting on the slope of the mountain-side above the Horseshoe Curve and watching the trains slowly panting upward or carefully sliding down the heavy grade. Apparently there is not an hour of the twenty-four, when one or more trains are not visible from this point. The sound of laboring locomotives and clanking couplings ceases not by day or night, year in or year out.

Aside from its importance as a division terminal, the town is still further distinguished by being the location of an immense system of railroad shops. It has, in fact, probably the largest railroad population in the world, numbering about seventy thousand inhabitants. The only other business of any size in the place employs not over one thousand workmen. All the miscellaneous industrial activities, such as those of the storekeepers, doctors, street-car employes, policemen, preachers, etc., must be credited to the railroad, as they serve the railroad employes, and without them they would be out of work. The Pennsylvania Co. has here an immense locomotive repair shop, a locomotive testing plant, car shops, and foundry; and a locomotive building plant at Juniata, a suburb toward the east. It is the practice in this latter shop which will be described in the following.

Shop Practice from the Juniata Plant

At the Juniata shops are built all the passenger engines for the Pennsylvania Railroad, and many of the freight engines as well. It takes a system the size of the Pennsylvania to build locomotives in sufficient quantities to make a shop of this kind profitable or possible. As it is, the types have been standardized and the work has been brought down to a manufacturing basis. The extent to which the interchangeable idea has been carried out would seem incredible to a mechanic not familiar with locomotive building, or familiar only with old-fashioned practice in that work.

In the present part of the complete treatise on locomotive building contained in MACHINERY's Reference Series Nos. 79 to 84, inclusive, attention will be given especially to the making of the main and side rods. The separate operations are comparatively simple and may be shown readily by photographs. Many of them are ingenious, however, and some of them have highly suggestive value for similar work in other lines.

The rods chosen for illustration are those for a heavy consolidation freight locomotive. A drawing of the main rod is shown in Fig. 3.

Fig. 1. Type H-8-B Consolidation Freight Locomotive built for the Pennsylvania Railroad at the Juniata Shops, Altoona, Pa.

It will be seen to differ radically in some particulars from the usual design. While the cross-head end is of familiar construction, the rear end catches the eye at once in looking at the finished locomotive. This is due to the placing of the key at the outside end of the rod. A rod made like this has an unfamiliar appearance, but its advantages grow on the beholder as he looks at it.

The construction is exceedingly simple, requires considerably less machining and a much smaller number of bolts and other small parts. It would seem to be secure as well. It will be noted that the key has a projecting lip at its lower end, which interlocks with a notch cut in the lower end of the bolt. This, in connection with the lock nuts on the bolt and the groove provided for the point of the set-screw in the key, makes it practically impossible for anything to get loose and fly out. To have this happen, the key set-screw would

Fig. 2. Finishing the Main Rod Forging under the Steam Hammer

have to be unscrewed, or the point broken off; the cotter pin for the lock nuts on the bolt would have to be sheared; both nuts would have to be loosened and fall entirely off; and then both bolt and key would have to be thrown out at the top of the opening. It will be noted that the channeling is parallel. This permits the operation of cutting it out to be performed at one setting for each side. The flanges of the section are thickened at the rear end, giving the necessary increase in strength.

Roughing Operations on the Main Rod

Fig. 2 shows the blank for the main or connecting-rod in the forge shop. This treatise deals with the machining operations particularly, so the forging will not be elaborated on. The picture is interesting, however, in showing the type of equipment provided in this plant. Attention should be called to the large, airy room and the fine lighting. The completed forging is shown in Fig. 4 mounted on the scales. The weight of the particular one shown was 1,985 pounds. This

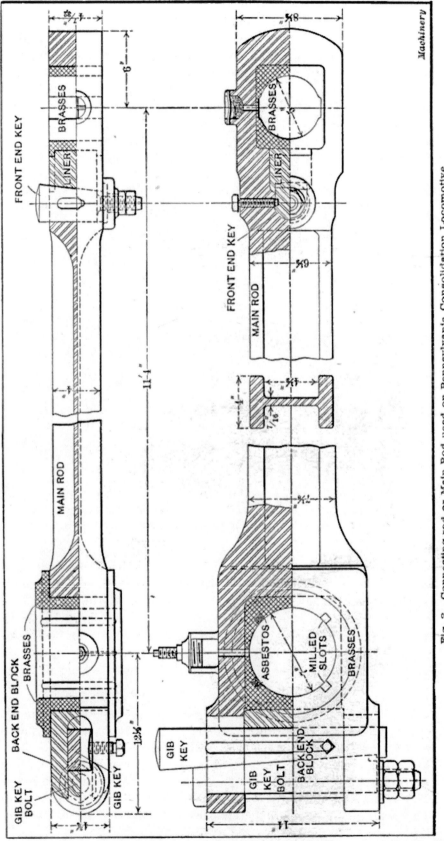

Fig. 3. Connecting-rod or Main Rod used on Pennsylvania Consolidation Locomotive

should be noted, as later on figures will be given to show the amount of metal removed in the different machining operations. It may be mentoned that the main rods, and all other parts of the locomotive, for that matter, look very much larger on the floor of the shop than they do when seen in place on the finished machine as it stands on the track. This ton-weight of forged steel is a very imposing piece of metal, indeed.

The first shop operation is that of planing the sides, top and bottom of the two heads of the main rod. The sides, in this operation, are planed down to size while the top and bottom are roughed only, these surfaces being of complicated form as may be seen from Fig. 3.

These cuts are taken on a planer of special design, widely used for this work. As best seen in Fig. 5, it has two sets of housings and cross-rails. Each set it provided with two tool heads on the cross-rail and two side heads, making eight tools available for simultaneous working. In the case shown all eight tools are at work.

Fig. 4. Weighing the Rough Main Rod Forging

The table of this machine is not provided with a quick return, since the tools on one end cut in one direction, while the others cut on the back stroke. The housings at the right of Fig. 5 are adjustable along the length of the bed to agree with the length of rod being machined, thus adapting them for intermediate and end rods as well as for the long connecting-rods here shown. Fig. 6 shows a rear view from one end of the machine, showing four of the tools at work. The four at the other end are set in similar positions.

After machining one face and one edge at each end, as shown in Fig. 6, the rods are turned over onto these machined surfaces to permit the finishing of the other face and other edge of each. The methods of holding the work are of the simplest, being those used in standard planer practice. The rough planing of these surfaces leaves the rods in a condition to be clamped to the table and to each other on machined surfaces for subsequent operations.

Laying-out and Finishing the Body of the Rod

The rods are now taken from the planer and placed on horses on the open floor, where a workman lays the templet on each of them

Fig. 5. Double-head Planer for Surfacing the Main Rod Ends

and scribes around it, on the planed faces of the two heads, the outline to which to finish the rod. Guided by these lines he prick-punches the centers for the various drilling operations required in working out the open and closed ends of the rod, and in machining the slots for the keys, bolts, etc. The laying out for all subsequent operations is all done at this time. By scribing from a templet in this way, assurance is given that the forging will finish out to the required size, and the work of taking measurements in machining is greatly reduced.

Fig. 7 shows the next machining operation, which is that of milling the top and bottom of the I-beam section of the rods. This is done, as shown, in a heavy slab milling machine with inserted tooth cutters, to which reference will be made in another part of this treatise. (See

Fig. 6. **Rear View of Planer showing Four Tools at Work on One End of Two Main Rods**

MACHINERY'S Reference Book No. 82, Locomotive Building, Part IV.) Four of the forgings are mounted in place on the machine at a time. The ends of each rod are blocked up to bring the surface to be milled horizontal and at the proper height, as indicated by the scribed outline on the work.

It will be noted that piece No. 2 shows evidence of having got into difficulties. The distortion shown, however, is evidence of remedial action, instead of being the original cause of the trouble. The workman found, in lining this piece up on the planer in Fig. 5, that there was not stock enough to finish out the open end of the rod to the full width. It was, therefore, sent back to the shop and swaged out in the center, as shown, which widened it to the required dimensions. The reduced portion in the center comes in the part which is cut out to receive the brasses, so that it still permits the head to be finished out to the required dimensions. The kind and amount of chips produced in this operation give evidence of the size of cuts taken on locomotive work in this shop. A copious supply of lubricant is, of course, brought to the cutting edges.

After milling each of the straight sides of the rods, as shown in Fig. 7, the operator works out, so far as he can, the outline of the heads at both ends as scribed by the templet. This is done by raising or lowering the cross-rails by hand as the table is fed past under the cutters, following the scribed line and working out the metal close to it. This operation naturally requires considerable skill on the

Fig. 7. Finishing the Top and Bottom Edges of the Main Rods
in the Slab Milling Machine

part of the operator in following the line as closely as possible without breaking through it. The result of his skill is shown in Fig. 10, where the forging, as it looks after this operation, is shown on the scales. It will be noted by comparing this with Fig. 4 that 485 pounds of metal have been removed so far.

The I-beam section has next to be formed in the body of the rods by the milling of channels on each side. This operation is shown in progress in Fig. 8. The same machine is used as shown in Fig. 7, using inserted tooth cutters of the proper dimensions with corners rounded to the radius of the inside edges of the channel. Two rods are laid on the table side by side, held by suitable stops and clamps.

Fig. 8. Channeling Operation performed with Inserted Tooth Cutter

The cutters for this operation are 8¾ inches in diameter, and they revolve at 36 revolutions per minute, giving a surface speed of 82 feet per minute. The table feed is 1⅝ inch per minute. Two cuts are taken over each channel to bring it down to depth, the cut being 4½ inches wide and about ⅞ inch deep for each cut and cutter.

The supplementary support for the cutter arbor between the two cutters was no part of the original equipment, being added in the shop. It was found to greatly increase the capacity of the machine. It is only in the past decade that mechanics have discovered how important in the matter of production, is a support for the tools and the work rigid enough to prevent the harmful vibration and chat-

Fig. 9. Cutting out the Jaws for the Open End of the Rod in a
Double-blade Sawing Machine

tering, which destroys the edges of cutting tools. The amount of metal removed in the operation shown in Fig. 8 is something over 500 pounds for each rod. The rigidity of the machine, the design of the cutters, and the proper relation between surface speed, feed, and depth of cut has a great deal to do with the efficiency obtained.

Working out the Jaws, Key-slots, etc., of the Main Rod

The rods are now taken to the drill press to drill the holes mentioned in the operation of laying out the work with a templet. For the rear or large end of the connecting-rod, the block taken out in forming the jaws is not removed entirely by drilling. As shown in Fig. 9, this block is cut out by a double sawing machine, the drill

Fig. 10. The Main Rod Roughed Out

holes being used beyond the extreme depth to which the saws can enter. The outer end of the rod is supported on a horse in this operation, remaining stationary, since the feed is applied to the head on which the saws are mounted. These saws are of the inserted tooth type.

Fig. 11 shows the condition of the rod at the end of the operation shown in Fig. 9. It also shows the various holes drilled from the

Fig. 11. The Main Rod ready for the Slotting Operations

lay-out provided by the templet. It will be noted that holes of various diameters are used. At the large end the large holes at the bottom of the jaws are properly located and of the proper diameter to furnish the rounded surface to which the inner corners of the opening are finished. In the same way the corner holes of the opening at the small end and the large holes in the key-slot are properly located and sized for finishing at these points. This accuracy in the laying out and drilling of these holes simplifies the finishing operations in the slotting machine very much.

Fig. 12 shows the slotter at work on the rear end of the rod. A tool is used having cutting edges rounded to the radius of the corners

Fig. 12. Finishing the Open End on the Slotting Machine

of the opening, so as to join easily onto the radius produced by the drill holes. Comparatively simple outlines are required, as is shown plainly in Fig. 3. The lines scribed by the templet furnish the guide to the operator in this operation. The same cuts for the

Fig. 13. Drilling the Hole for Keybolt Slot

small end of the rod are shown in progress in Fig. 14, which more plainly shows the form of tool used. This is provided with top rake as shown, and will cut when feeding in all four directions. A rubber tube for the lubricant is brought down close to the cutting point.

Fig. 12 and, later on, Figs. 25 and 31, show an interesting form of
cutter support for heavy over-hanging work of this kind clamped
to the slotting machine table. A horse or trestle is provided with
a pair of leveling screws, each supporting a roller. On these rollers,
as shown, is mounted a bar provided, in turn, with pivots for a
second long roller. On this the work rests. It will be seen that this

Fig. 14. Working out the Opening at the Cross-head End of the Main Rod

arrangement allows the work-table of the slotting machine to be fed
or adjusted in and out, or from one side to the other, without any
interference to this movement from the support of the outer end.
The work will roll freely in and out on the long upper roller, and
the bar on which that roller is mounted will roll freely from side to
side on the rollers mounted in the screws supported by the trestle.

After finishing out the openings as just described, the rod is taken
to the drill press, where the holes for the two ends of the key-slot
are drilled, as shown in Fig. 13. Fig. 15 shows this slot being worked
out with a tool similar to that shown in Fig. 14. A key-block, such
as is used in the finished rod, is mounted between the two ends of
the jaws, as shown, to take the strain of the cutting and the clamping

Fig. 15. Working out the Keybolt Slot on the Slotting Machine

in place so as not to spring the work. The outer end is supported as
in Fig. 12.

In the next operation the oil holes are drilled and counterbored
and the oil cup at the small end is worked out. This is rounded,
as shown in Fig. 3. The oil cup at the large end is not rounded at
the present time, as it is there shown, but is left in the shape of a

rectangular block the full width of the head as seen in Fig. 20. The only reason for rounding this oil cup would be to effect a slight saving in weight and appearance. It does not appear that the slight advantage is sufficient to warrant the cost of the operation.

The rod is now finished so far as the machining operations are concerned, and is in the condition shown in Fig. 16, where its weight

Fig. 16. The Main Rod at the Completion of the Machine Work

is shown to be 657 pounds. This, it will be seen, is only one-third of the rough weight of the forging as given in Fig. 4. This is an interesting example of the efficiency of modern machining operations. It would be possible to forge the blank much closer to size than is done in actual practice, so that the amount of metal removed could

Fig. 17. The Brasses, Liners, Gibs, Bolts, etc., to be fitted into the Main Rod

be greatly lessened. It is so simple a matter, however, to remove large quantities of metal with rigid machines and suitable tools, that there is no economy in taking the time required to forge close to size. As a consequence, twice as much metal is cut off and thrown into the scrap as is left in the finished part.

Bench Work on the Main Rod

The main rod now goes to the bench and vise operators, where it is polished and fitted to the parts that go with it, shown in Fig 17. The polishing is done (see Figs. 18 and 19) by emery wheels hung

Fig. 18. Suspended Emery Grinder used for Finishing

on counterbalanced swinging frames from the ceiling. These have entirely supplanted the laborious and time-consuming filing operations that used to be employed. The wheels can be manipulated so as

Fig. 19. Grinding and Polishing the Channels on the Main Rod
with Suspended Grinder

to follow flat and round surfaces with equal facility, smoothing out all the roughness of the outlining operations on the heavy milling machines. Fig. 18 shows the wheels smoothing up the round for the swell of the head at the open end. Fig. 19 shows a small wheel with a rounded edge finishing up the corner of the groove in the channel.

In addition to these polishing and finishing operations, the parts shown in Fig. 17 have to be fitted into place. The machine work done is of such a grade that no machine operations are required for fitting these pieces. A little easing with the file and the vise here and there is all that is required. The parts themselves and their uses in the rod will be readily understood by reference to Fig. 3. Fig. 20 shows the completed rod on the scales.

Design of the Side Rods

Fig. 28 shows the type of end rod, and Fig. 22 the intermediate side rod used on these consolidation locomotives. Owing to the short center distances between the crankpins, the inertia of the rod as it flies up and down is not so serious a matter as in the case of the main rod. For this reason, it may economically be made of a plain rectangular section as shown. Solid bushings are used, with no pro-

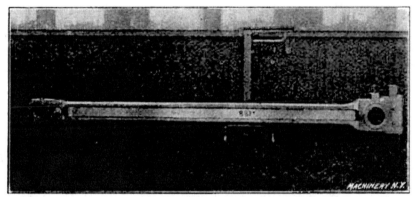

Fig. 20. The Main Rod ready for the Locomotive

vision for adjusting. When these are worn to a point where further use becomes inadvisable, they are pressed out and replaced with new ones taken from stock. Forked pivot-hinges are provided to which the end rods are connected with a knuckle joint, as shown best in Figs. 22 and 34. This is the usual construction for consolidation locomotives. Owing to the inequalities of the track and unequal wear of the driving wheel tires, there can be no assurance that the driving wheel axles will remain in the same plane, so it is necessary to hinge these rods to give a free vertical movement for the axles with relation to each other.

Split boxes have sometimes been provided for the crankpin bearing for one of the end rods, either the front or back, but this is not now done on this road. Adjustment of center distances is rendered unnecessary at the present time by the exceedingly careful attention to dimensions given in the shop. In machining and inspecting, the distances between the finished surfaces of the frame pedestals of the driving boxes are required to come right within the thickness of a piece of paper, which (as any mechanic knows) is somewhere near 0.005 or 0.006 inch at the most. Under such conditions, end adjust-

Fig. 21. Finishing the Sides of the Heads of the End Rods

ment becomes unnecessary. Such variation in center distances as results from wear affects alike the axle boxes and the crankpin bearing.

Removing the Metal from the Rod Forgings and Laying them out with Templet

In Fig. 21 is shown the first machining operation on the end rod. Two or four of these at a time are laid on the bed of the planer-type slab milling machine, while the side surfaces of the stub ends are worked off on one side. The forgings have, of course, been packed on the machine so as to rest firmly, and the depth of cut is so gaged as to leave stock to finish out on both the heads and the rectangular sections. The holding of the work is effected by the means common in planer practice, which have been found sufficient for the heaviest

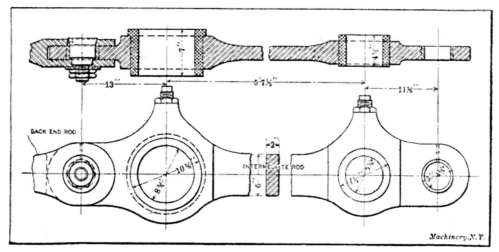

Fig. 22. Intermediate Side Rod

cuts on the slab milling machine. Of course the principal strain is against the back stops, and these, it will be seen, are of very heavy construction.

After milling both heads in the manner just described, these end rods are turned over to the templet man, who scribes out on them the outline, the location of the holes, etc., the same as was done for the main rod. They are then returned to the slab milling machine and milled on the top and bottom edges of the rectangular section and around the outlines of the heads, as described for the main rod in connection with Fig. 10, and as illustrated for the intermediate rod in Fig. 30. The templets for laying out these parts are shown lying beside the base of the milling machine in Fig. 23. One of them is for the front end rod and the other one for the rear, practically the only difference between the two being a slight variation in length.

Fig. 23 also shows the next machining operation, which is that of milling the sides of the rectangular section of the end rod. Four of these are mounted in the miller at a time, two cutters being used on the machine spindle. Substantial stops are provided, as shown, for the end-thrust, while the work is held to the table by straps which

Fig. 23. Finishing the Sides of the End Rods in a Slab Milling Machine

are moved as may be required to permit the passing of the cutters. After one side is completed, the rods are turned over and the other side of the section is milled.

Working out the Holes and Openings

The next operation is that of drilling the hole which forms the bottom of the cut made by the double sawing machine, in forming

Fig. 24. Cutting out the Knuckle-joint Slot in the End Rod

the slot for the hinged connection with the intermediate rod. The saws are shown cutting into this hole in Fig. 24. This is the same machine as shown previously in Fig. 9, at work on the main rods. The outer end of the work is supported on a roller mounted on a screw-jack and trestle for convenience in setting the work.

This is not required for the feed of the machine, which is applied to the saw-slide instead of the work-table.

The slot thus roughed out has next to be finished. This operation, shown in Fig. 25, is done on the slotting machine with the same arrangement of tools and fixtures as used on the main-rod operations shown in Fig. 12. The roller support for the outer end of the work is here shown to better advantage.

It will be noted by reference to Fig. 28 that these slots are tapered in to the center line of the hole, and have parallel sides from there to the bottom. This taper is comparatively slight, being only 1/16 inch in the whole distance. The tongue of the intermediate rod which enters this groove is similarly tapered at the outer end, and parallel at the inner end. This provides for a slight lateral flexibility in the separate members of the system of the rods. This is a very necessary provision, as it is not practicable to fit the driving wheel axles

Fig. 25. Machining the Knuckle-joint Slot for the End Rod in the
Slotting Machine

without end play, nor is it possible to keep them so fitted after they have been in service for a while. The circular table of the slotting machine comes into play in the cutting of the tapered portions of the slot. It is turned slightly to the right for one side of the slot, and slightly to the left for the other side, permitting the whole slot to be machined without shifting the work on the table.

The next operation is a very interesting one. It is that of cutting out the stock for the crankpin holes. These holes are not cut out of the solid, the operation being rather one of trepanning, as it has sometimes been called from its resemblance to the surgical operation occasionally performed on damaged skulls. The work is strapped to the platen of a special vertical double spindle boring machine, as shown in Fig. 26. This machine is powerfully driven by a motor at each end of the main shaft, and is provided with suitable feeds and speeds for rapid work in tough materials. The speed changes are

Fig. 26. Cutting the Crank-pin and Knuckle-pin Holes in the End Rod in a Double-spindle Newton Boring Machine

effected by variable speed motor control, while the changes in feed are made by a positive quick change gear device. As shown in the engraving, the tool removes a solid plug of metal from the hole, it being necessary to expend only the power required for removing a comparatively thin chip between this plug and the solid wall of metal in the work. Some of the removed plugs are shown in the engraving, lying on the rod, and piled at the end of the machine.

The style of tool used is shown in Fig. 27. As may be seen, two inserted cutting blades are used, mounted in a cast head of such form as to provide a strong support and at the same time to give ample chip room—a matter of importance in a cut of this kind. Each blade is located by a tongue resting in a groove cut in the holder. It is held in place by tap bolts passing through slotted holes, and an end adjustment is provided by set-screws passing through to the top of the holder. This permits the two blades to be set so that each does its share of the work.

The time required to cut out a plug for the 9⅞-inch hole in the
end rod in 50-point steel, 4 inches thick, is approximately 22 minutes.
The capacity of the machine was considerably increased by the support
given to the spindles close down to the work. This was designed
and added to the machine in the shop. As may be seen, these supports

Fig. 27. Type of Tools used in the Operation shown in Fig. 26;
these tools remove a Solid Core from the Hole

are adjustable lengthwise to follow the spindles in whatever position
the latter may be placed. Another convenience is the stops provided
on the cross-rail for locating the heads. These clamp firmly on the

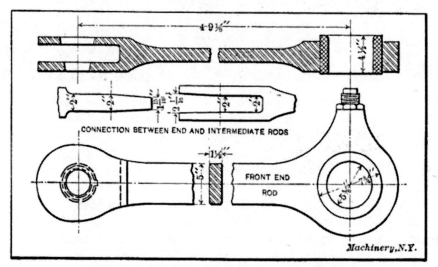

Fig. 28. Details of the Construction of the End Rod

lower **V** of the guiding surface and are adjustable to any position.
By means of them the heads may be shifted from one definite position
to another, so that the four holes met with on the intermediate rods
(as will be described later) are bored without taking measurements
on any except the first pieces set up. The holes in the rods thus

roughed out are finished in the same machine with suitable boring tools and reamers.

While the outline of the end rods has been in part roughed out on the milling machine, so much of this is circular as to permit its being finished very nicely on the vertical miller in the way shown in Fig. 29. The work is clamped in place on the circular table on

Fig. 29. Machining Circular Outlines of the End Rod on the Vertical Milling Machine with Rotary Table

the axis, first of the crankpin, and then of the knuckle-pin, while the contour in each cut is finished to the proper radius by the circular feed. On this same machine the remaining non-circular portions of the outline are worked out by hand in a way similar to that described for the main rod on the horizontal miller.

Fig. 30. Cutting the Edges and Outlining the Heads of the Intermediate Rods on the Slab Milling Machine

The subsequent operations for this piece resemble similar operations on the main and intermediate rods, so special reference will not be made to them. These operations include the drilling, counterboring, tapping, etc., of the oil holes, the polishing and finishing of the surfaces, the fitting of the brasses, etc.

Operations on the Intermediate Side Rod

The details of the intermediate rod are shown in Fig. 22. This has the same rectangular sections as the end rod, and requires solid bushings, simply pressed in place. The holes in the tongue for the knuckle-pin, connecting it with the end rods, are bushed with case-hardened and ground steel, bearing on a pin which is treated in the same way.

The operations are the same as for the end rods, up to and including the milling of the upper and lower surfaces of the rectangu-

Fig. 31. Finishing the Sides of the Tongue for the Knuckle-joint on the Intermediate Rod in the Slotting Machine

lar sections. Owing to the fact that there is comparatively little circular outline around the main crank-pin bosses, these are worked out on the slab milling machine by the vertical adjustment of the cross-rail by the operator as shown in Fig. 30, the operation being similar to that described for the main rods. The engraving shows the work set in place in the machine, but not yet clamped down. Care is taken in setting the work to have the outlines scribed by the templet come at the same height at each forging, so that the workman can do four at once and follow only one outline.

The next operation is the finishing of the sides of the tongues, where they fit into the slot in the knuckle-joint of the end rods, This is done in the slotter with a tool-holder which permits the blade to be relieved on the back stroke. The operation is shown in Fig. 31. The circular table is used as on the end rod to machine the tapered end of the tongue for the hinged joint. The rolling outboard support and the method of holding the work is plainly shown. The holes for the crankpins and joint-pins are worked out on the boring machine in the same way as shown in Fig. 26. The stops on the cross-rail are used for locating the spindles in shifting them from the crankpin to

Fig. 32. Milling Circular Outlines in the Intermediate Rods with the Outer End of the Work Supported from a Swinging Arm

the hinge hole, and *vice versa*, making repeated measurements unnecessary.

The finish milling of the circular portion of the outline of the rod is done as shown in Fig. 32 in an operation similar to that shown in Fig. 29. In this case, however, owing to the greater length and weight of the work, it becomes necessary to support it at the outer end.

This is done very handily by a crane swinging from a support on the top of the frame of the machine. While the center of the swing of this crane is not concentric with the axis of the table, it is near enough so that very slight adjustment is required in the length of the chain

Fig. 33. Re-boring the Bushings in the Intermediate Rods
after pressing them into Place

hoist to properly support the outer end, while it is swung around from one side to the other for the circular feed.

The rod is now ready for polishing under the suspended emery wheels previously described, and for having the solid bushings forced into

Fig. 34. Intermediate and End Rods assembled and
laid out for Inspection

place. This is done under heavy pressure, so that the bushings are squeezed together slightly, reducing their inside diameter. In order to bring them back to standard size again for the fit on the crank-pins, the rods are taken to the double-spindle boring machine shown in Fig. 33, where they are re-bored to size. Great care is taken, of course, to preserve the center distance, and to have the new holes exactly concentric with the old ones—that is, with the holes bored in the rod itself.

After the work of machining on the intermediate and end rods has been done, they are all assembled and laid out on horses, as shown in Fig. 34. Here they are inspected for all important dimensions. Rapid and effective work done in the assembling department of this plant demands great accuracy in the dimensions of the parts produced in the shop. This is the final examination of the work for accuracy in these dimensions and it is very carefully done.

Fig. 1 shows the side and main rods at the place of their destination mounted on a "Type H-8-B" freight locomotive, the heaviest engine built by the road. This is of the consolidation type, as shown, and weighs on the drivers 211,000 pounds and on the trucks 27,333 pounds, giving a total weight of 238,333 pounds. The cylinders are 24 inches diameter by 28 stroke, and the wheels are 62 inches in diameter. A boiler pressure of 205 pounds is carried, and the engine develops a tractive force of 42,660 pounds—a very satisfactory figure. In this type of locomotive it is not necessary to pare down the weight, so the parts have been made ample for all the strains that will be imposed on them. The result is a construction which was expected, and has so far proved, to be very durable and serviceable. It is probable that, if heavier freight locomotives are ever required for the road, recourse will be had to the Mallet articulated type.

MACHINERY'S REFERENCE SERIES

EACH NUMBER IS ONE UNIT IN A COMPLETE LIBRARY OF MACHINE DESIGN AND SHOP PRACTICE REVISED AND REPUBLISHED FROM MACHINERY

NUMBER 80

LOCOMOTIVE BUILDING

By Ralph E. Flanders

Second Edition

PART II

WHEELS, AXLES AND DRIVING BOXES

CONTENTS

CHAPTER I

WHEEL AND AXLE WORK

In MACHINERY'S Reference Series No. 79, "Locomotive Building—Part I," were described, step by step, the operations followed in making the main and side rods of a consolidation freight locomotive. In the following the same consecutive method will be followed in describing the machine shop work on the axles, wheels, centers, tires and crankpins, in the Juniata Shops of the Pennsylvania Railroad at Altoona, Pa. The finished product resulting from these operations is shown in Fig. 33, which illustrates the main driving wheels and axle of a new design of exceedingly heavy passenger locomotive, recently built. These are 80-inch wheels, the largest now used in regular pas-

Fig. 1. Raw Material for the Wheel and Axle Work

senger service. The locomotive, being of the Pacific type, requires three driving axles in all.

In Fig. 1 is shown a stock pile of forgings and steel castings in the yard outside the shop, from which the finished work in Fig. 33 is built up. The axles and pins are forged from nickel steel. The tires are made by the circular rolling process, and are received at the shops rough. The wheel centers are steel castings.

The Main Axles—Drilling and Inspecting Holes

Fig. 2 is a drawing of the driving axles of the K-2 Pacific type locomotive, giving the principal dimensions. As shown and as seen also in the axles in the pile at the right of Fig. 1, holes are drilled clear through the axle centers, the diameter of the hole being 2 inches in this case. The purpose of this hole is simply to permit inspection of the

interior of the forging. If there is a defect in an axle forging anywhere, it may be expected at the center, where seams due to piping
and other troubles would surely be found if they were present at all.
By examining the interior surface with an electric light mounted on
a long rod and provided with a reflector, it is possible to be assured
that each one of the thousands of driving axles used on the locomo-

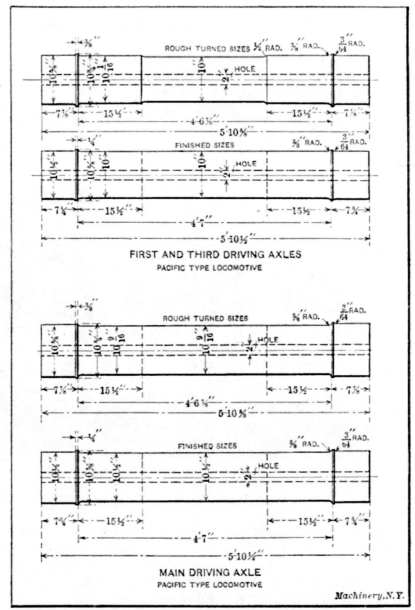

FIRST AND THIRD DRIVING AXLES
PACIFIC TYPE LOCOMOTIVE

MAIN DRIVING AXLE
PACIFIC TYPE LOCOMOTIVE

Machinery, N.Y.

Fig. 2.   Rough and Finished Turned Dimensions for Driving Axles

tives of the Pennsylvania system is flawless and homogeneous. This
is a form of insurance which is rather expensive, but it is exceedingly effective.

Two forms of axle boring lathes are shown in Figs. 3 and 4, the
first of these being the older design. In this machine, as shown, a
hollow spindle is used, large enough to take the work in bodily. This

is grasped by a chuck at the front end, and is centered and supported at the rear end on the points of three set-screws, so that it runs practically true. The drill itself is stationary, being grasped in a clamp bushing on a special carriage. The supporting bushing guides the drill close up to the work, starting it truly and keeping it in line until the end of the operation, thus assisting in keeping the hole concentric. The reason for revolving the work instead of the drill is, of course, that the hole can be kept concentric with the work when this is done. If the work were stationary while the drill only revolved, the chances are that the hole would run away out from the center line of the work, especially if it should meet a flaw or a hard spot in the metal.*

Now while it is necessary to revolve the work, it is evident that this involves constructional difficulties in the lathe itself. The spindle

Fig. 3. Drilling the Test Holes in the Axle Forgings

shown in Fig. 3 has to be of a very large diameter, and must be run at very high speed if it is to allow a modern inserted blade drill to operate to the best advantage. To overcome the necessity for revolving a large spindle at high speed, the improved form of axle boring lathe shown in Fig. 4 was developed. Here the spindle is of ordinary proportions, the work being held at one end in the chuck while it is centered and grasped at the other in a revolving holder of the "cat-head" type. This simplifies the problem by reducing the spindle diameter. Still further benefit is derived by revolving the drill itself at a high rate of speed instead of having it stationary as in Fig. 3. The work is also revolved, but all the beneficial results in the way of truing up the hole, can be obtained if the rate of revolution is quite slow. In the case shown, for a two-inch hole, the axle revolves at 15 revolutions per minute, and the drill in the opposite direction, of course, at 75 revolutions per minute.

---

*See MACHINERY'S Reference Book No. 25, "Deep Hole Drilling."

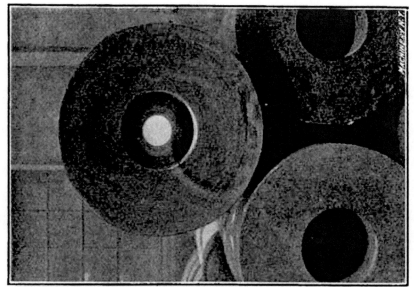

Fig. 5.   Test Hole under Inspection

Fig. 4.   An Improved Design of Boring Lathe for Drilling the Axles

The drill head is clamped to a regular lathe carriage, and is connected for driving the drill with a special splined shaft at the back of the lathe. Unlike the machine shown in Fig. 3, this is practically a regular engine lathe, with only the addition of this splined driving shaft, the drill head on the carriage, the bushing support for the drill, and the revolving rest for the front end of the axle. Otherwise it is provided with lead-screw, change gears, and all the other requirements of the standard engine lathe. It may be used as an engine lathe when the attachments are removed. It is motor-driven, with a controller operated from the carriage.

A well-known type of deep-hole drill is used for this operation. It consists, as shown in Fig. 6, of a long bar *A* of steel, with a slot milled across its front end, in which an inserted blade *B* of high-speed steel is held by means of a taper pin *C*. Square grooves are provided on each side for the escape of the oil and chips. In circular grooves on

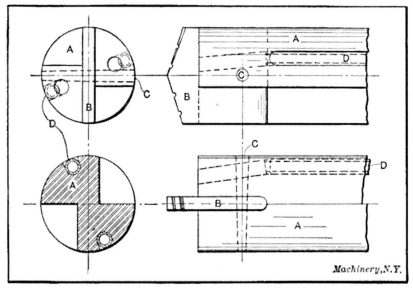

Fig. 6. The Drill used for Deep Boring in the Machines
shown in Figs. 3 and 4

the side, tubes *D* are brazed, which lead the oil from the socket in the lathe carriage through to the cutting point. The only part of this drill subject to ordinary wear and replacement, as will be seen, is the steel blade *B*, which is very simple and inexpensive. These lathes, of course, are provided with power pumps, settling tanks, etc., for handling the lubricant, which in this case is a soda-water compound. This is delivered to the carriage by a "trombone pipe" arrangement in the case shown in Fig. 4.

Fig. 5 shows one of the holes drilled and under inspection. For this purpose an electric light is passed in at one end of the bore, provided with a reflector so mounted as to shade the eyes of the inspector from the direct glare of the filament, and still show clearly the walls of the bore, by the reflected light. As these holes have been drilled for inspection and insurance only and are of no further use, they are promptly plugged up again to provide centers for the subsequent machining operations on the axles. Various methods of plugging have been tried; but the one which has proved the most satisfactory in the long run at the Juniata Shops is the method which is also the simplest—namely, that of reaming out the ends of the bore with a taper reamer and forcing in corresponding taper plugs in the wheel press. The reamer and the plugs have a taper of ¾ inch per foot. In

Fig. 7.   Forcing Taper Plugs into the Ends of the Bore of the Axle

Fig. 8.   Centering the Axle Preparatory to Turning

Fig. 7 the plugs are shown being pressed into place; a pressure of approximately 15 tons is used for this operation. The axles are now to all intents and purposes solid, and are treated as such throughout the remaining operations.

The axles are now ready for the turning operations, and the special machinery operations.

Finishing the Driving Axles

Fig. 8 shows the axle being centered. This is done in a special machine. The two ends are grasped in V-jaws tightened by right-and left-hand screws, which center the axle in front of two drill-spindle heads, one at each end. These heads are driven by bevel gearing from a splined shaft running through the center of the bed, and each is provided with a threaded quill and handwheel for feeding. As usual in centering, a leading hole is first drilled and this is then finished out to a center by the use of the countersink shown. The drift hole provides for rapid changes of drill and countersink.

From the centering machine the axles are taken to the lathe shown in Fig. 9, where the journals and wheel-fits are turned. Templets are used for the lengths of these cuts, one of these templets being shown laid on the wheel-fit at the near end of the axle. Fixed gages are also used for diameters. One of these is shown applied to the

Fig. 9. Turning the Axles

journal, while the other is lying on the top of the carriage. The journals are finished by the rolling operation shown in Fig. 10. The roll is mounted in a forked holder in the tool-post, and fed back and forth across the work under a considerable pressure. There is an opportunity here for the display of judgment by the operator in the matter of the pressure applied. This must be heavy enough to roll down the tool marks and harden the surface. If too great a pressure is applied, however, these results are not obtained; instead, the surface is flaked and disintegrated, leaving it unfit for use in the bearing.

A little kink in estimating the smoothness of a surface is worth mentioning. The instinctive way of doing it is to run the tip of the finger across it to see how it feels. A more delicate test, however, consists of running the edge of the thumb-nail over the surface. For some reason this shows up ridges and irregularities of the surface much more sensitively than does the flesh of the finger tip.

The axle is now taken to a special milling machine, where the key-seats are cut 90 degrees apart on the ends, the two operations being simultaneous. This machine is shown in Fig. 11. The construction of the machine is plainly evident. The axle is mounted on its centers, and is supported on V-blocks which in connection with the weight of the axle, serve to keep it from moving under the cut. Two sliding

Fig. 10. Finishing the Axle Journals with the Rolling Tool

Fig. 11. Keyseating the Axles on a Special Quartering Milling Machine

cutter heads are provided, with axes at an angle of 90 degrees with each other. This brings the wheels on each side of the engine with the crankpins exactly 90 degrees apart; in other words, it "quarters" the wheels.

The cutters on these spindles have to be accurately centered, of course, if the quartering of the keyways is to be accurate. For this

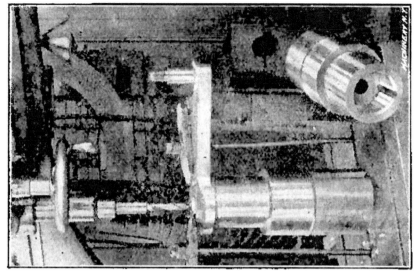

Fig. 14. Drilling the Dowel Holes for Locating the Return Crank

Fig. 13. Return Crank located in Proper Relation with the Keyseat

Fig. 12. Keyseating the Crankpin in the Horizontal Miller

purpose a center line is provided on the back slope of the teeth, half-way between the sides of the cutter. This line on the cutter, in the original construction, was lined up with a pointer set in a stud in a bracket provided for the purpose on the cap of the cutter spindle bearing. The seat for the stud is shown, though the bracket is not in place. This method of centering has been changed somewhat in the practice of the shop. Instead of using this pointer, a reference surface shown at *A* in the engraving is used on the tailstock, and the measurements are made from this to the face of the cutter to set it central. This would seem to be a very satisfactory method, as it would not be affected by wear in the slides and changes in the tightness of the gibbing, owing to the fact that the reference point or surface is directly mounted on the member which supports and centers the work.

After the keyways have been cut on this machine the axle is ready for assembling with the wheel-centers.

Finishing Operations on the Crankpins

The crankpins are machined from the rough forgings by obvious chucking and lathe operations which do not need to be described in detail. With the Walschaerts valve gear, these pins are of two kinds, depending on whether the Walschaerts crank is to be screwed and doweled into a counterbore, as in the case shown in Fig. 14, or is to be keyed and bolted with a split hub, onto a seat turned on the outer end of the pin, as for the case of the K-2 wheel shown in Fig. 33.

The pins shown in Figs. 12, 13, and 14 are of the former sort. Fig. 12 shows the operation of milling the keyseat for the fit of the pin in the main driving wheel center. This keyseat is, of course, required for the main pin only, as this is the pin from which the valve gear connections are made. The other crankpins are forced into place without keying. In Fig. 12 the work is simply held between centers in an ordinary horizontal milling machine, and the keyway is cut with a mill properly centered. At *B* is a key, set into the keyway of a templet mounted just back of the pin; it is used merely to indicate the existence of the templet, which is out of sight. The latter has on it a line corresponding with one scribed on the pin, with which the Walschaerts return crank must match. This templet is used, therefore, in locating the keyway with reference to the line of the crank.

In Fig. 13 the crank has thus been properly located. In Fig. 14 it is shown on the drill press while the three dowel holes which locate it with reference to the pin are being drilled. These holes, as shown, after passing through the flange of the crank, are drilled half into the hub of the crank and half into the counterbore of the pin, locking them firmly together. The crank itself is, of course, held in place by a bolt passing through the center of the pin, and fastened by a nut on the inner face of the wheel.

Boring the Tires

In Fig. 15 is shown a section through the driving wheel rim and tire. The method used on the Pennsylvania R. R. for holding the tire in place is clearly shown. The usual lip or shoulder is provided on

Fig. 16. Boring the Tires Two at a Time in the Wheel Lathe

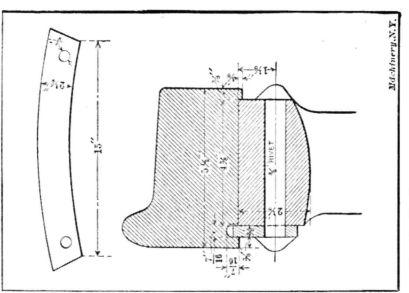

Fig. 15. The Tire and Its Retaining Ring

the outer edge of the tire for taking the heavy thrust of the rail against the flange of the tire in rounding curves, taking switches at high speed, etc. In addition to this, a groove is turned in the bore of the tire and into this is set a series of plates about 2¼ inches wide and 15 inches long, as shown, held to the inner face of the wheel rim by ¾-inch rivets. Six of these plates are ordinarily used, spaced equally around the rim.

This provision for locking the tire in place is made necessary by the tendency which tires have to loosen from the centers under certain conditions. It is a common occurrence to have a tire so heated by the slipping of the wheels on the track in starting at heavy loads, that it will loosen from the center and start to slide off. It cannot, of course, come clear off, as it is retained in place by the flange striking against the rail. The tire is shifted from its position, however, and when it cools again the gage of the engine has been widened, necessitating a cautious trip to the shop for reheating and replacing the tires. By the use of various methods of locking, of which the clip arrangement here shown is one of the most satisfactory, this difficulty is avoided.

The tires are received from the rolling mills rough all over. The finish rolling is, however, accurately and smoothly done. The first operation consists in boring the tire for its fit on the wheel center, and also for forming the retaining lip or shoulder. This operation may be done in either the wheel lathe or the boring mill. In Fig. 16 the tires are being bored in the lathe. They are held on the faceplate by clamps and blocking, and are mounted on parallels to provide clearance for the boring tools when working at the extreme inner edge. The tire is located in place for clamping and is accurately centered by a set of stops with adjustable screw-points, located between each of the four clamps shown. The operations of boring, and of forming the lip, are all of an obvious kind and do not need to be described in detail. An interchangeable blade boring tool is used. The inside diameter is accurately turned to a standard length gage.

Operations on the Wheel Centers

The wheel centers shown in Fig. 17 are of cast steel. Two forms of counterweights are used. One style shown in this figure is cast solid with the wheel centers. This is the style commonly used on passenger wheels of large diameter, where it is possible to get a large enough weight and one far enough from the center to produce the required balancing effect. On freight engines, in general, where the wheel is very much smaller in diameter, it is not usually possible to get into the required space enough weight in cast iron. On this account such counterweights are ordinarily cored hollow, and poured full of lead so as to get the required weight in the required space.

Instead of pouring this into an enclosed space, the Pennsylvania practice is to pour it into open chambers, as shown plainly in the freight wheel in Fig. 20. After these have been poured full, a plate of steel is bolted on for a cover, preventing any possibility of the

Fig. 18. Pre-heating the Wheel Center while Melting the Bronze for the Hub Liner

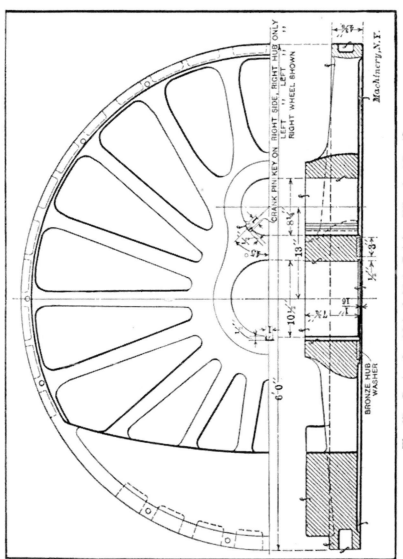

Fig. 17. Center for 80-inch Main Driving Wheel of Pacific Type Locomotive

lead being lost out. The advantage over the closed chamber lies in the fact that in the latter case, the interior is difficult to clean properly and difficult to fill properly; it is common for the lead filling to shake loose and to rattle around as the wheels revolve.

The first operation, if the wheel is to have a hub liner or washer, is the turning of the seat for this with dovetailed grooves to hold

Fig. 19. Boring and Turning the Wheel-center

it in place. This is done on the boring mill. The pouring of a bronze liner that will not crack while it is cooling is an operation that many railroad shops have difficulty with. The method here followed, however, obviates this trouble entirely. The secret of success is shown in Fig. 18, where the wheel-center is seen mounted on horses directly over the crucible oil furnace in which the bronze is being melted. The hub of the wheel is not merely warmed, but is heated to a high degree, being somewhere near the point where it would begin to show redness. When the bronze is poured into the heated hub, the liner and the hub shrink together, so that the cracking of the former is entirely obviated. It may be said that the cracking of the liners does no particular harm, it being, in fact, common custom to use them in this condition; but certainly the cracking does them no good, and when it can be avoided by a simple process like this the little extra trouble is worth while.

The wheel-center is now taken to the boring mill, and is first mounted with the inside surface uppermost. Here the periphery and the inside edge of the rim are faced and the hub bored and faced. The wheel is then turned over and mounted as shown in Fig. 19. Here the outside edge of the rim is faced, as is also the hub and its exten-

Fig. 20. The Counterweight Poured into Open Chambers

sion for the crankpin. The center is shown between the two operations in Fig. 20, which also shows very plainly the open form of chambers provided for receiving the counterweight lead in freight locomotive practice.

The particular wheel here illustrated is intended for the electric locomotive on the New York Tunnel service. It will be noted that only the two outside chambers are filled with lead. This particular casting is intended for the rear wheel, in which only the weight of the side-rod is to be balanced. If the same casting were to be used for the main driving wheel, the weight of the connecting-rod from the jack-shaft would also have to be balanced, requiring all the chambers to be filled with lead. This construction permits the use of one casting for both styles of wheels, thus simplifying the question of patterns, and making the castings, in a way, interchangeable.

The hub surface of the axle and crankpin is next marked with chalk, as shown in Fig. 21, for scribing the keyways for the axle and the pin. A templet is used for this operation, two forms of which are shown in the engraving. The one in place is for the K-2 or Pacific type locomotive, in which the return crank for the valve gear is located at the proper angle by the keyway of the crankpin. The templet consists of a cross made of rectangular steel, provided with

Fig. 21. Laying out the Keyseat for the Crankpin with Special Templet

Fig. 22. Keyseating in the Slotting Machine with Special Squaring Plate for Setting the Work

gage marks and a circular segment for locating it on the axle bore, and with a disk templet, as shown, for scribing the crankpin bore and marking the keyway. Of the four projections on this disk the two shown nearer the axle are for the keyways, that on one side being used for the right-hand wheel, and the one on the other side for the left-hand wheel.

For lighter types of locomotives, the crankpin keyway is put directly in line with the axle keyway, both being on the connecting center line. For this condition the templet shown lying against the wheel is used. This is located in the axle bore in the same way, and the crankpin bore is scribed. The long steel bar to which the other members are fastened is the width of the key used in both bores, so this is used for scribing their location. For locomotives using the Stevenson gear, no keyway is required for the crankpin, of course; so only the axle keyway and the crankpin hole are scribed, to insure proper quartering.

When the keyways have been thus laid out, the wheel center is taken to the slotting machine, as shown in Fig. 22, where the keyways are cut to the lines scribed in the previous operation.

For those centers where the keyways are in line with each other and on the center line of the axle and crankpin, great assistance is given in the matter of setting up by the plate shown at *C*. This is

Fig. 23. Pressing the Axle into the First Wheel

fastened to the face of the column of the machine by studs, and is carefully set so that its surface is exactly at right angles to the ways on the bed, on which the work-table is adjusted in and out. By setting a square against this accurate surface, the wheel-center to be machined may be set so that the two keyways exactly square up, and are thus in line with the ways of the machine. When the tool is right for cutting one keyway, the work may be shifted over to cut the other without further setting.

The next operation, not illustrated, is the drilling of the various holes required for the tire retaining plates, the counterweight cover-plate, etc. After this operation, and the pouring of the counterweights, the center is ready to be forced on the axle.

Assembling the Wheels, Axles and Tires

The wheel-press is shown in use in Figs. 23 and 24. The first operation shows the press immediately after the forcing of the axle into the first center. The axle is supported from the tie-bar in the usual sling, accurately set for height by means of the screw adjustment shown. The wheel center rests on a roller support, by means of which it may be turned until the keyway exactly lines with the key fitted in the axle.

Fig. 24 shows the second center being forced on. This is also mounted on a roller support for bringing the keyway in line with the key. Blocking is used, as shown, so that the ram applies its pressure to each side of the hub, forcing it down to its seat on the axle, and allowing the end of the latter to project through it slightly if its length is such as to require this.

For a 10-inch wheel-fit like this, the axle is turned approximately 0.010 inch larger than the bore of the hole in the center, the usual rule being about one-thousandth inch allowance per inch diameter of fit. An axle of this size would require anywhere from 120 to 145 tons

Fig. 24. Pressing the Second Wheel onto the Axle

pressure to force it home, this pressure varying with the character of the machining on the surface fitted and with the exact dimensions to which the parts are finished.

The wheels are now ready to have the tires shrunk on them. Where this tire-shrinking job is done on the wholesale as it is, for instance, at the Altoona repair shops, a heating furnace is used into which the tire is set bodily. In continuous operation this arrangement heats a great number of tires per day. For establishments where the operation is only occasional, the favorite arrangement is to provide a pipe slightly larger in diameter than the tire, and provided with a series of jets through which a gas flame is directed on the tire around its circumference. For the number of tires per day, however, which have to be attended to at the Juniata shops (one locomotive per day is the regular capacity) the arrangement shown in Fig. 25 has been found entirely satisfactory. It provides for heating the tire uniformly around its circumference with a single flame, this flame being so arranged as to be capable of accurate control and to give an economical and efficient flame.

As shown in the engraving, the arrangement consists of a turntable on which the tires are mounted, a combustion chamber of sheet iron lined with fire-clay, and a burner in which crude oil is atomized by compressed air at the regular shop service pressure. The combustion chamber is swung on a swivel, as shown, so that it may be directed properly against the work. The burner is supported by it, and is supplied by flexible pipes. The tires are mounted two at a time on the turntable, which is slowly revolved by a push from the operator every once in a while. To determine when the tires have reached the proper heat, an inside solid gage is used, similar to the one used for boring

Fig. 25. Heating the Tires on a Turntable for Shrinking onto the Centers

the tires in Fig. 16, but larger, of course, by the amount of expansion the tire must possess before it can stretch over the wheel-center.

When it has expanded to the point where the gage will enter the bore of the tire in any direction, the tire is picked up by the crane and dropped on the floor of the shop. The crane then picks up the axle with the two centers and drops one of the centers into the tire. The second tire is then picked up and dropped onto the upper wheel-center, the combination being left in the position shown in Fig. 26 until the tires shrink on. The centers and tires rest against the lip on the latter, of course, so that they shrink squarely into position. The chalk mark "H" on the lower tire means that the tire is hot. The correctness of this statement could, without doubt, be determined by experiment.

After the tires have cooled down so that they are firmly shrunk into place, the wheels are taken to the quartering machine shown in Fig. 28, where the crankpin holes are bored. This well-known tool bores the crankpin holes exactly 90 degrees from each other. This is, of

Fig. 26. Shrinking the Tires onto the Centers

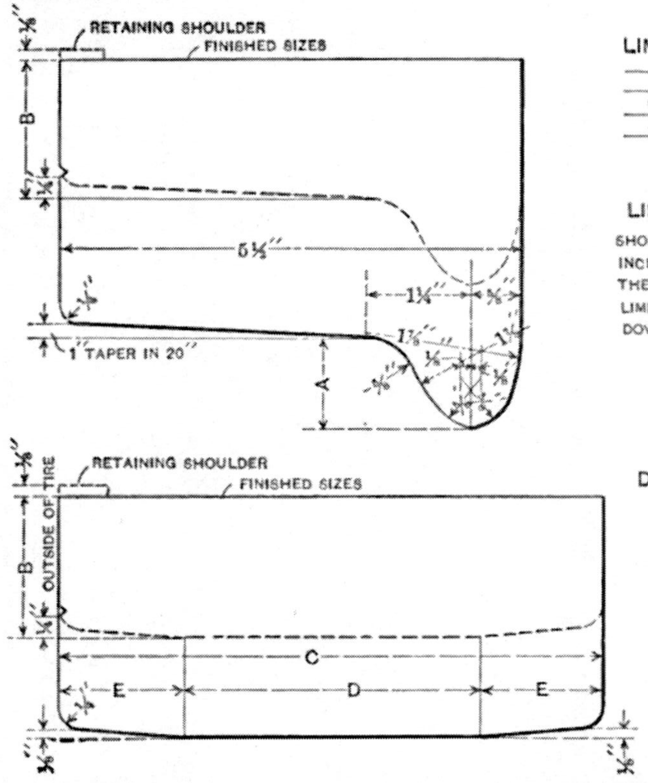

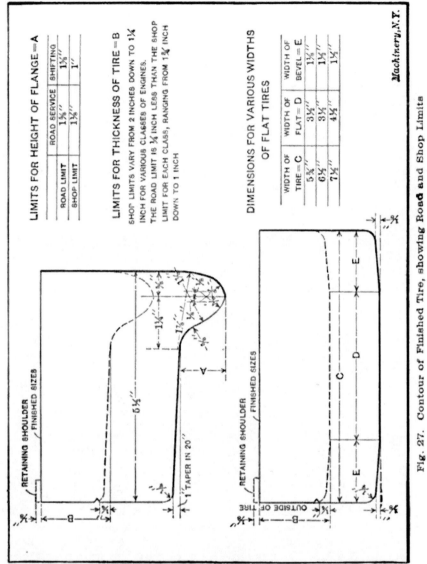

LIMITS FOR HEIGHT OF FLANGE = A

	ROAD SERVICE	SHIFTING
ROAD LIMIT	1⅜″	1⅜″
SHOP LIMIT	1⅛″	1″

LIMITS FOR THICKNESS OF TIRE = B

SHOP LIMITS VARY FROM 2 INCHES DOWN TO 1¼ INCH FOR VARIOUS CLASSES OF ENGINES.
THE ROAD LIMIT IS ¼ INCH LESS THAN THE SHOP LIMIT FOR EACH CLASS, RANGING FROM 1¾ INCH DOWN TO 1 INCH

DIMENSIONS FOR VARIOUS WIDTHS OF FLAT TIRES

WIDTH OF TIRE = C	WIDTH OF FLAT = D	WIDTH OF BEVEL = E
5¾″	3½″	1⅛″
6½″	3½″	1½″
7½″	4½″	1½″

Machinery,N.Y.

Fig. 27. Contour of Finished Tire, showing Road and Shop Limits

course, a matter of great importance, for if the various pairs of driving wheels are not all accurately quartered, with crankpins at exactly the same radius, they will cramp and bind in the connecting-rod brasses, until these are distorted or worn loose enough to allow for the inaccuracy. If the quartering machine is accurately made, the wheels may have their crankpin holes bored in them with perfect confidence that they will run properly under the locomotive.

The axle is located by its centers, as in the case of the axle keyseat milling machine shown in Fig. 11. On each end of the bed two heads are mounted, one on one side and one on the other, adjustable for the throw of the crank; each carries a boring spindle as shown. Between the wheels are furnished outboard bearings for the boring-bars, permitting heavy cuts to be taken without vibration or chatter, and without danger of inaccuracy. The rims of the wheels are clamped to this support, as shown, to hold them firmly in position. If the quartering of the keyways in the axle, and the slotting of the keyways in the hubs of the driving wheel, are properly done, the outlines scribed on the crankpin hub at each end can be accurately finished out by this boring operation.

If the wheel cannot be set so that the crankpin holes, as bored by the machine, will finish out to the line on each wheel, it is evident that the keyway on the hole that does not finish out will be out of place, throwing the pin around, and therefore disturbing the relation of the return crank which operates the Walschaerts valve gear. A check is thus furnished for all preceding operations, so far as they refer to the valve gear. It is not expected, and indeed is not found, except in rare cases, that the preceding operations have been at fault, but wherever they have been, notice is served of the difficulty in time to make such corrections as may be required before the engine is assembled. It should be noted that the keyway is filled with a dummy key, approximately flush with the cored hole, before boring the crankpin seat. The operation is not so hard on the tool as it would be for the blade to pass through the open keyway at every revolution.

It will be seen that the quartering machine is arranged so that the boring slides can be mounted on the opposite sides of the heads from that shown, if desired. This makes it possible to quarter wheels in which the right side leads, as well as those in which the left side leads. Engines are now made with the left side leading as standard practice, but some of the older designs, which have to be reckoned with in repair work, call for the right side leading. Provision also has to be made for this in the axle keyseating machine shown in Fig. 11. Here it is not so much trouble to change the machine over, as the milling heads are simply fed along the slides until they have passed each other and are working on the opposite ends of the axle. The feed-screws are long enough to permit this.

Turning the Tires

Another operation, shown already performed in Fig. 30, is the turning of the tires, which is done in the wheel lathe in which the

Fig. 28. Boring the Crankpin Holes in the Quartering Machine

Fig. 29. Finishing the Ends of a Gang of Crown Brasses in a Double-spindle Milling Machine

tires were bored, in Fig. 16. All passenger locomotive tires are turned on centers the last thing before the crankpins are forced in place, before the wheels are sent to the erecting floor. On freight locomotives, which do not run at so high a speed and are not so hard on the track, the tires are simply centered very carefully for the boring, finish turning not being required.

The standard contour for driving wheels on the Pennsylvania

Fig. 30. The Wheels ready for the Crankpins

Fig. 31. Forcing in the Crankpins

system is shown in Fig. 27, which also gives details as to the road and shop limits for the height of the flange and the thickness of the rim. Whenever one of the flanges wears down below the road limit given for dimension A, the wheels are brought into the shop to be turned off again. When this has been done so often that another turning would reduce dimension *B* below that given for the shop limit, the tires are scrapped. Whenever dimension *B*, in service, wears below the road limit given for that dimension, the tire is scrapped. The measurements for determining dimension *B* are taken from the V-groove shown turned in the outer face of the tire, which is ¼ inch below the minimum limit. This groove is cut into the tire in the wheel lathe during the turning operation. Dimensions for flat tires with the various limits are also given in Fig. 27.

Driving the Crankpins and Finishing

Fig. 31 shows the operation of forcing the crankpins into place. In this operation the thrust of the ram against the wheel is taken care of by backing the latter against the "post," which is adjustable to the proper position on the top and bottom tie bars. This gives a solid backing for the pressure required to force the pin in place. About 0.008 inch allowance for driving is made on a crankpin fit

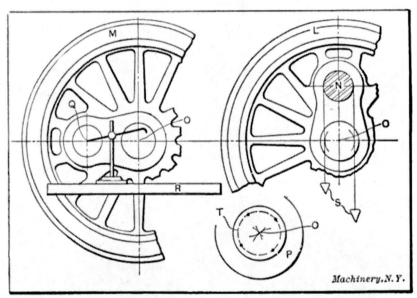

Fig. 32. Method of Testing and Quartering

of 8 inches in diameter, the pressure required ranging from 75 to 100 tons. It may be mentioned in this connection that the driving pressures for all axle and crankpin fits are recorded at the shops, and put on permanent record for use in case of any question arising as to the service of the engine on the road. The engraving shows the second pin being driven, the first having already been forced into place by an identical operation.

It was stated that an accurate quartering machine will take care of the proper boring of the crankpin holes without requiring any anxious thought in this matter on the part of the workman. It is, however, well to know how to test the quartering, so as to make sure that the machine is right in the first place, or to make sure that it does not for any reason wear out of line as time goes on. Fig. 32 shows how this testing is best done. The two wheels on the same axle are shown at *L* and *M*.

The first thing to do is to set the wheel so that crankpin N is exactly vertical over the center of the axle. This is done, as shown, by hanging a double plumb-line over the crankpin and rolling the wheel slightly one way or the other until it is located in position so that the center of the axle O is exactly equidistant between the two lines, or until the crankpin circle, struck with the dividers from center O, just touches the two plumb-lines equally on each side. Of course, in locating the center O, the axle sould be prepared the same as is customary for tramming in setting the valves. For this purpose, the center hole should be pounded full of lead and a new fine center accurately located on it. At the Altoona shops this center is located from a proof circle T turned with a sharp pointed tool on each end of the axle, while it is still in the axle lathe as shown in Fig. 9. By striking with the dividers from this proof circle as shown in the

Fig. 33. Completed Driving Axle and Drivers for Heavy Pennsylvania K-2 Type Pacific Passenger Locomotive

detail P, the center may be accurately located. Where it is not customary to turn a proof circle on the axle end, a ball point divider is used to scribe the proof line before the center is plugged up. Arcs are struck as shown from this proof circle until they intersect at the center, which is then marked with a prick punch. It is more accurate, however, to turn the proof circle T at the time the journals are turned.

Having set one side with the pin exactly vertical over the axle this way, the other side, shown at M, should be exactly horizontal with the center. To prove this, first set up a table having a surface-plate R mounted on it. With a precision spirit level, the best obtainable, bring this surface-plate to an accurate horizontal position. Then by means of a surface gage, test the center Q of the crankpin and O of the axle to see if they are the same height. The centers of both the pin and axle on this side should, of course, have been filled with lead and accurately centered in the same way as previously described, and as shown at *P*. If the lines on the vertical and horizontal sides have been proved to be correct by this method the wheels are properly quartered and the machine has done its work properly.

It is of great importance that the man in charge of the wheel work should know that the quartering machine is in good condition. If he is sure of this, he can meet with confidence the various reports of inaccuracies and difficulties in this particular that are sure to come to him from engines in actual use. He can meet such "kicks" with calm assurance, knowing that while something is doubtless the matter, it is not the quartering that is at fault.

The wheel, after being painted, is now ready for the assembling floor. The method of construction here described, it will be seen, makes use of the ordinary tools of the railroad shop and represents "good practice." Attention should be called particularly to the fact that fixed gages are used for all the important operations. This relates to the diameters of journals and axle fits, the boring of the tires, the turning of the wheel centers, etc., and besides this, as was explained, the use of the templet method of marking the keyseat and the bore of the crankpin furnishes an automatic check on all of the most important operations of the series.

CHAPTER II

DRIVING BOX MANUFACTURE

Among the great variety of manufacturing operations to be found in a locomotive building shop, the making of the main bearing boxes is one of those worthy of detailed illustration and description. The operations as laid out in the Juniata shops have proved to be efficient and accurate, but at the same time inexpensive in the matter of the

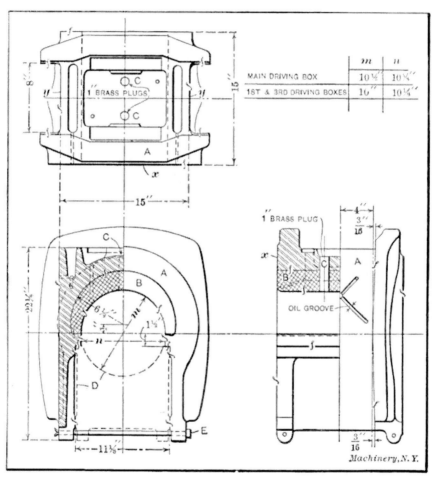

		m	n
MAIN DRIVING BOX		10¼"	10¼"
1ST & 3RD DRIVING BOXES		10"	10¼"

Fig. 34. The Main Driving Boxes for a Heavy Pacific-type
Passenger Locomotive

outlay for special tools and special machinery. Only standard machine tools are used on this job, such as find a large range of usefulness in the railroad shop. The number of special appliances is reduced to a minimum. For this reason the lay-out of the operations requires as high a grade of ingenuity as is needed for devising expensive special appliances for rapid manufacturing. In the description, we will begin with the machining of the various separate parts, proceeding therefrom to the assembling and machining of the finished product.

The Design of the Driving Box

A typical locomotive driving box is shown in Fig. 34. This design is used on an exceedingly heavy Pacific type locomotive. The box is of simple construction, consisting of but two parts, the driving box casting itself, A, and the crown brass B, which is driven into place in a machined seat where it is pinned by the two brass plugs shown at CC. These effectually prevent its loosening under any conditions. The cellar D, is indicated by the dotted lines only. The cellar used is a patented device of special construction, whose manufacture is a separate matter from that of the remainder of the box. It is held in place by two pins E.

This design of driving box has a plain finished face at x for the wheel thrust. The wheel itself has a bronze liner, which forms a suitable surface for contact with the steel casting face at x. Some

Fig. 35. Enlarged View showing the Two Inserted Tooth Mills

of the boxes shown in the following engravings, however, have a bronze liner inserted in surface x. Some of these liners are shown in Figs. 39 to 42. These are used when the hub of the driving wheel is not lined, but is simply faced up true on the steel surface. Still another method of treating surface x is to groove it out and pour a babbitt lining, on which a true bearing surface is faced. The standard practice here is to put bronze liners on the boxes, for the reason that it is more difficult to replace a liner on a wheel than on a box. Furthermore, when mounted on the wheel, the liner detracts from the length of the fit between the wheel and axle. This should be noted in connection with Figs. 49 and 50.

Machining the Crown Brasses

The first operation on the crown brasses or bearings, which are made of phosphor-bronze, is shown in Figs. 29 and 35. They are mounted, eight at a time, on long parallels on the bed of a duplex milling machine. An ordinary angle-iron serves to take the thrust of the feeding at the end as shown. The castings are held down on the parallels by simple bolts and straps in the central T-slot of the table, each strap spanning the distance from the top surface of one brass to that of the next. The strap of the first brass has, of course, as shown in Fig. 35, to be blocked at the outer end. In setting these up, the parallels are first lined up with the T-slot of the table, to serve as a gage. Then the separate brasses are put in place with the bolts between them, and packed solidly up against one another and against the angle-iron at the end, and set so that all of them project over the parallel the same distance; this leaves about the same amount of metal to be removed from all of them in finishing the ends. As each brass is put in place, care is taken to see that it is at right angles with the face of the parallels, a square being used for the purpose.

Fig. 36. Turning Two Crown Brasses at once on a Special Arbor

After being properly set and tightened down in this position, the cutter-heads are adjusted to the required distance apart, dividing the chip equally between each end of the work. The cut is then taken across as shown.

The next operation is that of turning the outside diameter of the brasses for the fit in the seat on the main bearing casting. This is done in the engine lathe, as shown in Fig. 36, on a special arbor whose details are shown in Fig. 37, and which permits turning two at a time. The special advantage of this arrangement is that the two brasses are set halfway round from each other on the arbor so that the lathe is cutting all the time. This is not so hard on the lathe as is the case when only one is being turned so that the single tool is "cutting wind" half the time. It also gives more rapid production, as two pieces are cut in practically the same time as one with former appliances.

In Fig. 37, which shows details of the device, the arbor carries a fixed flange in the center. The two brasses to be machined are clamped against the opposite faces of this flange by nuts and washers. Each, it will be seen, is thus clamped in place separately, and either member can be loosened without loosening the other. This construction is imperative in the matter of handling these heavy parts and clamping them in place in the lathe without the help of a laborer. The brasses are clamped on their faced ends, and are supported and lined up by means of "cat heads." There are two of these for each brass, and each has three bearing points for the inner surface of the work, set to line up the periphery properly, so that it will finish out when it is bored in place in the main casting.

Originally it was proposed that a special double carriage lathe be provided for this work. All that was found necessary, however, was to mount a supplementary slide on the carriage of an old lathe, and provide this with a second toolpost, as shown in Fig. 36. For this

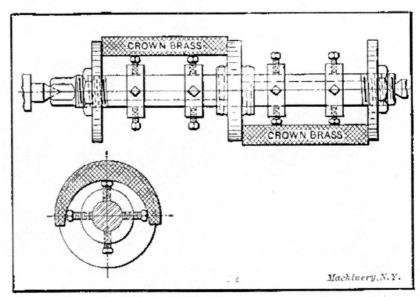

Fig. 37. Details of Special Arbor and Supports used for Turning Crown Brasses

work the arrangement is as satisfactory as a more expensive two-carriage lathe would be. The total time required for taking roughing and finishing cuts on two of these crown brasses is twenty-two minutes.

The final finishing operation on the brasses, before forcing them into the bearings, is that of milling the edges to fit the retaining lips in the bearings. The form is given these edges by means of two formed and relieved milling cutters, as shown in Fig. 38. These are both mounted on the arbor, at the same time, with an overhead support between them to reduce the chattering. A knee-brace is also used, as shown. The work is clamped down to V-blocks, each of which is provided with a hole for the passage of the bolt for clamping them in place, there being a bolt between each adjoining pair of brasses. A gage is provided of the exact contour of the outside and edge of the work, to which the brasses must fit after this cut has been taken.

Allowance is made in this gage for the extra stock required for the force fit for assembling them in the bearings. The time required for each brass on this milling operation is seven minutes.

Operations on the Bronze Thrust Liner

As previously explained, most driving boxes are provided with bronze thrust liners. The first operation required on these liners

Fig. 38. Milling the Edge of the Crown Brasses for the Fit in the Main Bearing Casting

Fig. 39. Facing the Bronze Liners for the Hub Bearing, on a Faceplate provided with Special Jaws

is shown in Fig. 39. This consists in facing the two sides of the phosphor-bronze liner casting. For this work the faceplate of an old lathe was equipped with the simple appliance shown. These appliances consist of three chuck jaws for gripping the outside of

Fig. 42. Machining the Bore of a Stack of Liners on the Slotter

Fig. 41. Slotting out the Cellar-fit in a Stack of Liners

Fig. 40. Turning a Stack of Liners on the Boring Mill, after Facing

the casting, an adjustable support or spreader for keeping the ends from springing together (as shown, this is operated by a right- and left-hand screw), and a three-bearing centering support in the inside of the casting, clamped in place by the central nut and washer. These simple devices hold the liner firmly in place for facing off front and back. One chip only is taken on the back side, with one roughing and one finishing chip for the bearing side of the liner.

In Fig. 40, the next operation on the liners (that of turning the outside) is shown. This is done on the table of the boring mill without special fixtures. The boring mill has a great advantage over the lathe, where work is to be done in stacks, as in this case. It is possible to locate the work and clamp it in place without difficulty, as there is no tendency for it to fall off the faceplate onto the floor while it is being set and clamped.

The top liner of this pile has been scribed with a templet to the outline desired. This outline is set so as to run concentric with the tool point, and the pile is squared up on its outside edges to match it, so that they all finish out alike. This operation includes two cuts, one roughing and one finishing.

The next operation consists in machining out the interior outline of the liner. This is also done in multiple, a stack of thirty-two being machined at once in the case shown in Fig. 41. As before, the upper liner has had the desired outline scribed upon it, and the circular interior surface or edge has been centered with the axis of rotation of the work-table, the whole pile being carefully lined up with this upper piece by means of a square, set on the table. The work being thus clamped in place, the jaws and lip are first finished out to the required outline (see Fig. 41), and then, as shown in Fig. 42, the rotary feed is applied, and the inner circle is cut out to the desired radius.

First Operations on the Driving Box

The first operation on the main driving box itself consist in machining out the fit for the crown brass. This operation is done on the circular table of the slotting machine, as shown in Fig. 43. The table having been set so that the tool point gives the proper radius, the work is mounted square with the table, and in a position which permits the interior to be machined out, allowing stock all around as well, as determined by a templet laid on the upper surface. The diameter of the crown brass fit, and the depth of cut at the retaining lips are made to match a templet having the exact contour of the crown brass, with suitable allowance for the force fit.

While set up in the slotter for the operation shown in Fig. 43, the workman scribes a line with the surface gage on the face of the casting on each side, at the same height all around. This line is used for the next operation, shown in Fig. 44, which is that of facing the back of the casting in the boring mill. This is being done in the nearest of the three mills shown. By setting the casting up to the scribed lines, the squareness of the facing with the seat for the crown brass is assured. The bearing is then turned over onto this faced

Fig. 44. Facing Operations on the Main Bearing

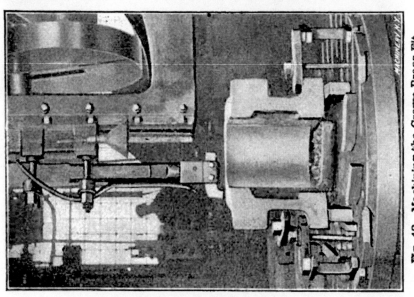

Fig. 43. Machining the Crown Brass Fit

seat and the outer face with the recess for the liner is machined. Where babbitted thrust surfaces are to be used, this surface is grooved for retaining the babbitt. The total time required for facing both sides, including counterboring and grooving, is two hours.

The work is slotted in this manner before facing, for the reason that the slotting is the vital operation, and the one where there is the greatest liability of not having stock enough to finish out. At the same time the facing, when it is to be counterbored for a bronze liner, must be concentric with the crown brass fit. For this reason it is safest to slot out the fit as the first operation.

Laying-off and Planing the Bearings

The first assembling operation is that of forcing the crown brass into the bearing. This is done under the hydraulic press as shown in Fig. 45. The crown brass is driven in at this time, before the planing operations, for the reason that the pressure of forcing the brass into place springs the bearing casting somewhat, so that it would not be safe to machine it beforehand. The workman consumes about nine minutes per piece in this operation. The castings with the brasses in place are now taken to the laying-off table, where, by means of a templet located by the projecting outside edge of the crown brasses, a line is scribed across the front face of the bearing. This is used in setting up in the operation of planing out the shoe and wedge fits for the frame pedestal.

For this operation, the work is set up on the planer table, as shown in Fig. 46. A large rectangular box casting forming a sort of angle-plate is clamped to the middle of the planer table, with its sides parallel to the ways. To each face of this casting are bolted and strapped six bearing castings as shown. Each of these is shimmed up from the table so that the line scribed in the laying-out operation just mentioned, is parallel with the platen, and at the same distance from the top of the table on all the castings, as shown by the surface gage. When the bearing castings have been set up on each side of the double angle-plate in this way, the grooves for the shoe and wedge fits on each side are planed to the proper width and distance from the front face, and to the proper height from the reference lines scribed by the templet.

The groove for the shoe and wedge fit, of course, is tapered 3/16 inch from each side as shown in Fig. 34, to allow the locomotive frames to rock on the springs without cramping the boxes. To obtain this double taper, each of the bearings is next loosened from position while a parallel shim of the proper thickness is inserted between it and the face of the angle-plate, at what will be the lower end when it is in place on the locomotive. They are then all clamped down again in this position while the planer tools rough out one-half the taper on each side of the slot of each casting. Then the castings are again loosened up while the shim is removed and changed so as to block out the work at what will be the top end of the casting. The work being again clamped down into place, the reverse taper on

Fig. 46.   Planing the Shoe and Wedge Fits in the Main Bearing

Fig. 45.   Forcing the Crown Brass into the Bearing

each side of each slot is worked out. This finishes the slots on one side.

In the next operation the bearings are all turned over and the shoe and wedge fit slots planed on the other side. In this case there is no packing underneath them, nor elaborate setting to be done, as they are simply clamped against the face of the double angle-plate and are squared up by resting on parallels placed between the finished shoe and wedge fit and the top of the table. As before, the double taper to permit the rocking of the engine on the axles and the springs is effected by shimming out first one edge of the box and then the other, on the double angle-plate. The total time on each bearing casting for planing the shoe and wedge fits, with the tapers for the rocking motion, is about three hours.

Miscellaneous Operations

Each box has now to be laid out accurately for the cellar fit, and for boring the crown brasses. This is done by the use of the templet

Fig. 47. Laying out the Cellar-fit and Bore on the Bearings

and scratching gage shown in Fig. 47. The face of the scratching gage, shown at *A*, is laid against the bottom of the finished surface of the shoe and wedge fit, while a line is scratched with the scriber along the knife edge *B* on the face of the box liner. Templet *M* is then laid on the face of the casting, and lined up by the mark just scribed. The scriber is again brought into play, and the lines for the bore and for the cellar fit are drawn on the face of the bearing.

In Fig. 48 one of the bearing castings is shown mounted on the table of the slotter for machining the cellar fit. It is mounted on parallels, of course, to allow clearance for the slotting tool. This machining operation simply consists in slotting to the lines scribed by the templet, and to the proper width to fit the cellars. This operation, on a large bearing, takes about one and one-half hour.

The next operation consists of facing the thrust surface, if babbitt is to be used, or in driving the liner into place if a phosphor-bronze surface is desired. This having been done, the face of the bearing is finished off in the boring mill. This is being done in the middle machine of the three shown in Fig. 44, which happens to be at work on an engine truck bearing instead of a main bearing. The time required for this operation is about nine minutes per piece.

A variety of holes for different purposes have to be drilled in the bearing, with its liner, crown brasses and cellar, which is now fitted into place. These various holes (oil holes, bolt holes, dowel holes for retaining lining, etc.), require about three and one-half hours complete. This varies somewhat, depending on whether hard grease or oil lubrication is to be used.

Boring the Boxes

The next and final operation is that of boring out the bearings. This is done in a double-table boring machine, as shown in Figs. 49

Fig. 48. Machining the Cellar-fit in the Slotter

and 50. It might be asserted, in connection with the opening remarks of this chapter, that this is a special machine. It is so in a sense, as it has a number of special features, consisting principally in the extended length of table used, and in providing two tables instead of one, with an intermediate bushing support. But these features are as applicable and useful in everyday boring practice, where a number of small or medium sized parts have to be handled, as for this particular work; so it is hardly fair to call this a special boring machine for this particular work.

As shown in Fig. 49, four bearings are bored at once, with a multiple blade boring-bar. The tables are long enough so that while this operation is in progress the workman can be removing and replacing four other pieces of work at the other end of the tables. There is thus little or no lost time in the operation of the machine. The workman is kept busy.

Fig. 49. The Last Operation. Finishing the Bearings on the Boring Machine.
Note use of Air Drill for Traversing Double Table

Fig. 50. The Work Completed. Finished Bearings ready for Removal from Boring Machine

As is also shown in Fig. 50, the work is clamped down onto parallels in the shoe and wedge slots, and it is located as well against parallels extending lengthwise of the tables for squaring up the work with the spindle of the machine. The lines scribed by templet M in Fig. 47 are relied on for setting the table of the machine to the proper height in beginning a lot of bearings, and also in adjusting each particular bearing to the proper position on the table. For this, measurements are taken from the end of the table to the scribed line on the face of each bearing, and all are made uniform.

Fig. 49 also shows another ingenious feature—namely, the use of an air drill in traversing the table from one extreme to the other, when changing from a finished to a rough set of castings. This distance is so long as to be tedious, when a change is made by hand. By hitching an air drill to the cross-feed, however, it is shifted very rapidly and easily.

This operation of boring the boxes is performed at the rate of fifty-five minutes per box. This includes rounding the corners of the bearing, as shown, and also the boring out of the cellar to the same radius and the same round. The completed work is shown in the foreground of Fig. 50. This is the last operation. At its conclusion the bearings are ready for assembling in the finished locomotive.

The time given on the various operations takes account of setting up the machine, taking measurements, and all other necessary but "non-productive" periods.

MACHINERY'S REFERENCE SERIES

EACH NUMBER IS ONE UNIT IN A COMPLETE LIBRARY OF MACHINE DESIGN AND SHOP PRACTICE REVISED AND REPUBLISHED FROM MACHINERY

NUMBER 81

LOCOMOTIVE BUILDING

By Franklin D. Jones

PART III

FRAMES AND CYLINDERS

CONTENTS

Copyright 1912 The Industrial Press, Publishers of MACHINERY

49-55 Lafayette Street, New York City

CHAPTER I

MACHINING LOCOMOTIVE FRAMES*

The frame of a locomotive might appropriately be called the foundation or backbone, as it holds in position the driving and reversing mechanism, spring rigging and other important parts which form the running gear. The complete frame is composed of right and left sections which extend longitudinally from either the cylinders or "bumper" at the front, to the foot-plate at the rear of the fire-box. These sections are not always composed of one continuous piece, but are often formed of two or three parts which are joined or spliced together by tightly fitting taper bolts. The general arrangement of the frame depends, of course, upon the design of the locomotive. When the frame is erected, the two sections or halves are bolted to the cylinder castings and they are further stiffened and held in alignment by cross-ties and braces. This matter of bracing is very important, as a rigid structure is necessary to withstand the severe strains to which the frame is subjected. As the driving wheels are held in position by the frame, the latter not only receives heavy fore-and-aft thrusts, but also severe lateral strains, especially when the locomotive strikes a curve at high speed; consequently, if the frame is weak and yielding, a fracture is only a question of time, and, from the beginning, there is likely to be more or less trouble with the driving wheel journals and rod bearings because the running gear is not held in alignment. Designers have had considerable difficulty in providing adequate frame braces on locomotives equipped with the Stephenson valve mechanism, because of the room required between the frames for the eccentric rods, links, etc. This difficulty, however, has been largely overcome by the extensive use of the Walschaerts valve gear which is located entirely outside of the driving wheels and permits braces to be used without interfering with the valve motion, at a point where they are needed most.

The machining of a locomotive frame would be a rather difficult proposition for the average machine shop, because of the size of the work and its unwieldy proportions, but in a modern locomotive shop, the operation is commonplace. At the Juniata shops of the Pennsylvania Railroad, the methods of handling this class of work are of exceptional interest, principally because of the high standard of efficiency maintained for the various machining operations. While this work is comparatively rough, if judged by the toolmaker's standards, considerable accuracy is necessary for certain surfaces, but the framework from start to finish is particularly noteworthy as an example of rapid machining rather than skillful and accurate work. The Juniata shops have, under normal conditions, a capacity for building a complete locomotive every day, and this rate is sometimes exceeded, so that the

MACHINERY, Railway Edition, March, 1912.

Fig. 1. Planing Two Frames simultaneously on a Powerful Planer equipped with Five Tools

machining of frames is an everyday occurrence. Practically all of the locomotives built in these shops at the present time, are equipped with cast-steel frames instead of wrought-iron frames which were used almost exclusively a few years ago. Frames that are cast are much cheaper than the forged type, and another advantage of using cast steel is that pads or other projections can be easily and neatly formed on the frame pattern.

Straightening and Planing the Frames

The cast-steel frames are usually warped more or less as they come from the foundry, owing to unequal cooling, and it is necessary to

Fig. 2. Where the Warped Frames are straightened prior to Machining

straighten them prior to machining. This straightening is done under a large steam hammer as indicated in Fig. 2. The frame is heated sufficiently to insure a permanent "set" when straightened, and it is made approximately straight by giving it a few blows with the hammer. The work is then ready for the first machining operation which is that of planing the sides and edges. Two frames or sections are planed simultaneously on a very rigid planer having five tool-heads. A view of this machine taking a roughing cut over the sides of two frames is shown in Fig. 1. The work is held on the platen by screw-stops and toe-dogs or "spuds" which are placed in an inclined position to force the work down. Stops are also set against the frames at the most advantageous positions to take the longitudinal thrust of the cut. Part of the time, all five planing tools are at work, the three tool-heads on the cross-rail being used to plane the sides of the two sections, while the right and left side-heads plane the edges. The three upper tools are started so that each rough planes about one-third of the surface formed by the two castings. In this way the roughing is, of course, done in much less time than would be required if an ordinary two-head machine were employed. As many of these castings have spongy, sandy spots, blow-holes or similar defects on the cope side, a generous allowance is left for planing in order to remove all porous material. Owing to the power of this machine, very heavy cuts can be taken without difficulty, as indicated in the illustration Fig. 1. The planer is motor-driven, and momentarily as much as 90 horsepower is required

Fig. 3. Cast-steel Locomotive Frame on its Way to the Shop

for driving, owing to the heavy "hogging" cuts which are taken in the tough cast steel. When roughing, the tools frequently cut to a depth of from 1/2 to 3/4 inch with a feed of 3/16 inch. The average depth of cut for the five tools, however, would be somewhat less than the figures given. After the three heads on the cross-rail are started, the right and left side-heads are set for planing the edges. The work is set up for rough planing the first side, with the top edge of each section outward. This is done so that the top edges can be finished with reference to pads for braces or brackets which are located on the inside of the top and bottom rails of the frames. After the roughing cuts on one side are completed, the finishing cuts are taken with broad flat tools which are given a feed varying from 1 inch to 1¼ inch per stroke. Only two of the cross-rail heads are used for finishing, so that each frame can be planed by a continuous cut in order to obtain a smooth surface free from ridges. The frames are next turned over for rough-

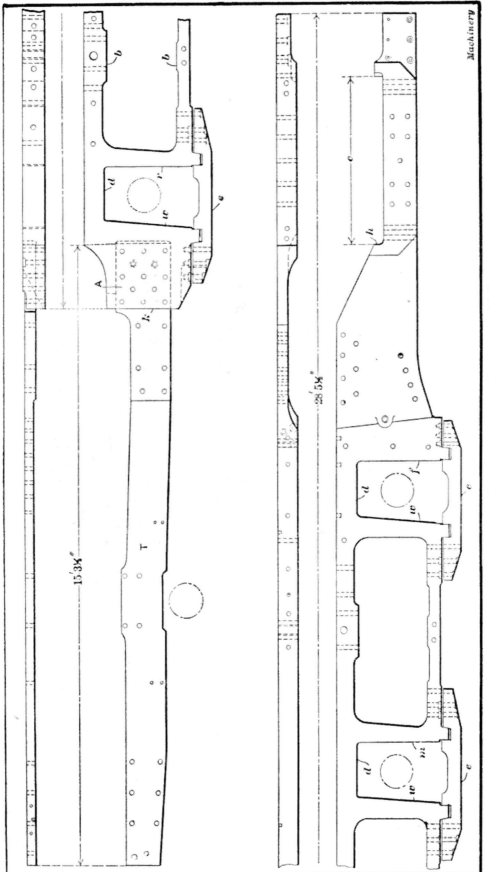

Fig. 4. Frame for a Passenger Locomotive of the 4-6-2 Type

ing and finishing the opposite side, reversing the position of the work illustrated in Fig. 1. The opposite edge of each frame is now in the outward position, thus permitting the ends of the pedestals to be rough planed. The finishing tools are set for planing the second side by means of a post or height gage to which the cutting edges are adjusted. In this way the proper thickness is quickly obtained, although a fixed caliper gage is used to check this dimension. After the sides have been finished in this manner, a frame of the type illustrated in Fig. 4 is planed at *A* for the reception of the trailer frame *T* which fits into a pocket as shown. This pocket, in turn, is finished to the correct width and depth in another machine. This completes the planer work.

Fig. 5. Frame mounted on Horses for Laying-out Operation

Laying Out the Frames

The frames are next laid out for slotting, though this operation is only necessary for every fifth or seventh frame (depending on the size) owing to the method of slotting them in stacks, as will be explained later. The work is placed on horses (as shown in Fig. 5) and steel templets are used to give the required outline. One of these templets conforms to the shape of the pedestal jaws and another gives the outline for the cylinder fit at the front end. Before placing the templets on the frame, the surfaces on which finished lines are to be scribed, are moistened with water and then coated with a soft red stone called "keel." This leaves a dull red finish on which the scribed lines are easily seen.

The templets are aligned by the planed edge of the frame and enable the required outline to be quickly scribed on the finished surface. A number of bolt holes which cannot be drilled to good advantage by the use of jigs are also laid out by the use of templets which have small holes corresponding in location with the holes to be drilled and these are transferred to the work by using a light punch. After the templet is removed, two concentric circles are stamped around each center with special punches similar to those shown in Fig. 6. These punches have V-shaped annular ridges which form neat rings or grooves, one of which represents the size of the hole while the other remains as a "witness" to show whether or not the hole has been drilled central. The punches are made in various sizes and they are much superior to the old method of scribing and dotting a circle, when laying out holes.

Slotting the Frames

The slotting operation, which is the next in the regular order, is performed by the large machine shown in Fig. 7. A stack of from five to seven frames (the number depending on the size), can be slotted simultaneously, so that it is only necessary to lay out the one which is

Fig. 6. Special Punches used for Laying out Holes

to be placed on top. As the illustration shows, the machine has three slotting heads. These can be traversed longitudinally along the bed by power and each slotting ram has a rapid power cross-movement, so that different heads can be easily and quickly adjusted to the required position. In setting up a stack of these frames, each section is placed against angle-plates at the rear which are in line with the slotter bed. All the frames are first adjusted longitudinally in order that the faces of all jaws will true up when the top frame has been planed to the lines previously scribed. The crosswise position of the work is then checked by testing the alignment of the lower frame with the bed. When this lower section is accurately located, the frames above are set by it in a crosswise direction by using a large square.

This slotting machine is operated by two men who proceed with the slotting operation in such a way that the three heads are used simultaneously as much as possible. The method of machining a stack of three-jawed frames similar to the type illustrated in Fig. 4, will illustrate how the machine is handled. One man begins slotting the shoe face *m* of the middle jaw, while the second man is rough planing the pocket *c* for the cylinder. When the first man has slotted the face of jaw *m*, he moves to the front and begins slotting shoe face *f*. In the meantime, the second man starts a finishing cut over surface *c*, and then begins work on the bracket pads *b* with the third head. The

Fig. 7. Large Three-head Slotter used for Slotting the Jaws of Locomotive Frames

reason the first man moves from the central jaw to the front, is that he is then in a position to watch the slotting head which has been started on a finishing cut along pocket *c* by the second man. In this way the two men shift from one point to another, the order of the operations depending, of course, on the arrangement or design of the frames being machined.

Fig. 8 is a detailed view, showing one of the three slotter heads. The slotting ram and its reciprocating mechanism is carried by a slide *S* which can be traversed laterally along the cross-rail shown. The rapid-traverse movements of this slide and also the power movements for shifting

Fig. 8. Detail View of One of the Slotter Heads—Seven Frames
are being Slotted simultaneously

the entire head longitudinally along the bed, are controlled by the vertical levers *L* seen at the left end of the cross-rail. This view shows the slotting tool just beginning a cut across the front or shoe face of the jaws. After the shoe faces *f*, *m* and *r* (which are square with the top of the frame) have been sotted, the tapering wedge faces *w* are finished. As those familiar with the construction of locomotives know, one side of the frame jaws is made tapering to provide an adjustment for taking up lost motion between the driving-wheel boxes and the frame shoes. It might also be mentioned, incidentally, that the rear jaws are given this taper rather than the front ones, because the latter are subjected to a greater pressure when the engine is running ahead, and it is better to have this pressure against a vertical surface than one that is tapering. The taper or wedge side is planed, on this particular slotter, by

Fig. 9.   Horizontal Milling Machine on which Trailer Frames are Milled

swiveling the cross-rail, on which the ram is mounted, to the required angle as indicated by suitable graduations. The slotting operation also includes the finishing of the top surfaces *d*, as well as the lower ends of the pedestals for the braces *e* which are bolted across each pair of jaws. In order to strengthen the frames, all corners have large fillets, and when these are being formed the slotting tools are turned by swiveling the tool-bar about its axis, the handwheel *W* (Fig. 8) being used for this purpose.

The most important part of frame slotting, from a standpoint of accuracy, is that of planing the square shoe faces, which must be finished the right distance from each other, within close limits, because

Fig. 10. Eight Trailer Frames set up for Milling the Edges

these are the surfaces which determine the location of the driving-wheels when shoes of a standard thickness are used. Gages are used for measuring these distances, the front and rear jaws being gaged from the central one which is machined first. The distance between shoulder *h* and face *f* is also carefully gaged, as this shoulder bears against the cylinder saddle and determines the longitudinal position of the frame. The jaw faces of the right and left frame sections must lie in the same plane and any irregularity in the location of shoulders *h* would affect the position of the jaws. The end *k* of each main section is also finished to provide a surface for locating the jig used for drilling the bolt holes for the trailer frame splice. Surface *k* is machined to a given distance from face *r* as shown by a fixed gage.

Milling the Trailer Frames

One of the most interesting operations on the frames is that of machining the section *T*, Fig. 4, called the "trailer" or rear frame.

Of course, it will be understood that these trailer frames are only used on locomotives of the passenger type having trailing wheels, which differ from the drivers in that they simply carry weight and are not connected by the side-rods. The trailer frames are forged and they are finished on the sides and edges in the powerful horizontal milling machine shown in Fig. 9. These forgings are not made very close to the finished size, because with the improved milling practice, the metal is removed so rapidly that it would not be economical to forge too close to the finished dimensions. The amount of metal removed in

Fig. 11. End View of Trailer Frames and Milling Machine

machining these frames is indicated by the fact that a rough frame weighs about 2212 pounds, whereas one that is finished weighs only 1725 pounds. The frames are first milled on the sides, two being placed on the machine at one time as illustrated in Fig. 9. The work is shimmed up with liners or thin wedges and held by ordinary clamps as shown. A stop-bar is placed across the outer end to take the thrust of the cut. As the milling cutter advances, the clamps are shifted from one point to another. The cutter used is 33 inches wide, and when the edges are being milled, practically the entire width of this cutter is in use. It consists of three 11-inch units having inserted blades which are held in accurate helical grooves, giving a constant cutting angle for the full width of the blade. These cutters are made in the Juniata shops and they are partly responsible for the efficient milling practice in connection with frame and rod work.

After both sides of all the frames in a lot have been machined, the edges are milled to the proper contour. At the present time, eight of these frames are milled on the edges simultaneously. The way the work is set up is indicated in Figs. 10, 11 and 12. Two broad clamps are placed across the top and the frames are held laterally by screw-stops along the sides. The rear clamp is provided with eight set-screws which insure a bearing on each frame section. The outer frame on the operator's side has lines showing the required outline for the finished edges. These lines are transferred from a steel templet before

Fig. 12. Stack of Trailer Frames blocked up for Milling Taper End

the frames are placed on the machine. The frames are first set up as shown in Fig. 10, and are then turned over for milling the opposite edges. As section F, Fig. 13, and middle section I, are tapering, it is necessary to block up the work as indicated in Fig. 12, in order to secure a straight tapering surface. This particular illustration shows the frames set for milling the tapered end F, Fig. 13. The irregular outline at the center and the radius at the wide end, are formed by adjusting the milling cutter vertically by hand as the work feeds forward.

In order to show how rapidly these rough forgings are machined to the proper size and shape, we shall give the actual time required for milling the various surfaces of the frames and the approximate depth of the cut. The various surfaces to which the data refers are marked in Fig. 13 by letters, and the lengths in each case are also given. Part A having a length of 5 feet 8½ inches is milled in 56 minutes, and the average cut varies in depth from ½ to ¾ inch. Of

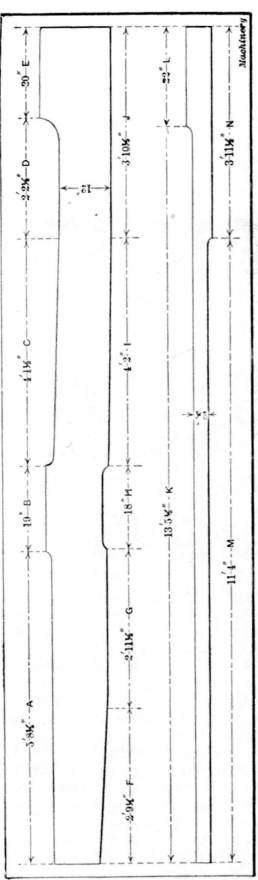

Fig. 18. Diagram showing Lengths of Milled Sections—Data covering Time and Average Depth of Cut is given in Text

course it will be understood that the time specified is for eight frames, so that if we only consider one frame, section A is milled in 7 minutes. The time taken for section B is 21 minutes and the depth of cut varies from ¾ to ⅞ inch; section C is 1 hour 6 minutes, depth of cut ¾ to ⅞ inch; section D, time 43 minutes, depth of cut ⅝ inch; section E is finished by planing prior to milling operation; section F, time 1 hour 40 minutes, depth of cut ½ to 2½ inches; section G, time 28 minutes, depth of cut ⅜ to 1 inch; section H, time 41 minutes, depth of cut, 1½ to 2½ inches; section I, 34 minutes, depth of cut ¼ to ⅞ inch; section J is finished by planing; section K, time 1 hour 15 minutes, depth of cut ⅛ to ½ inch; section L is finished by planing; section M, time 55 minutes, depth of cut ⅛ to ¾ inch; section N is finished by planing. The time given for milling the sides K and M is for two frames. The amount of metal removed from the edges of the eight frames is approximately 1356 pounds, whereas 2542 pounds are removed from the sides, giving a total of 3898 pounds. The total time required for milling the edges is 6 hours 29 minutes and for the sides, 8 hours 40 minutes, giving a total cutting time of 15 hours 9 minutes for eight frames, so that the amount of metal removed per hour of cutting time is approximately 257 pounds. It should be mentioned

Fig. 14. Gang of Three Radial Drilling Machines used for Locomotive Frame Work

that the foregoing figures do not cover the time required for setting and clamping the work on the machine.

Drilling and Finishing the Frames

There are a great many parts attached to the frames, such as brackets for the spring and brake rigging, stiffening braces, pedestal braces and many other parts, all of which require bolt holes, so that the drill press work is quite extensive, as is indicated in Fig. 4. Three large radial drilling machines are used for this work. The frame is first set up for drilling all the side holes, as shown in Fig. 14, and it

Fig. 15. Rounding the Corners of a Frame prior to Erecting

is then placed in a vertical position for drilling the pedestal-brace bolt holes. Most of the holes are drilled by the use of plate jigs which are located by previously machined surfaces and, in some instances, by lines drawn for this purpose when the frame is laid out. High-speed steel drills are used and these are flooded with soda water so that very rapid work is possible. As it is important to have accurately fitting frame bolts, the various holes are finished by reaming at the time the frames are erected, as will be described later.

After the frames are drilled they are removed from the machine shop to the erecting department, as the work has now progressed to the point where it is ready for assembling. Before referring to this last step in connection with the framework, attention should be called to the fact that all of these different operations are performed progressively, the work being advanced from one machine to the next without making any retrograde or backward movements. This is also true of other classes of work, the machines being arranged, as far as possible, so that the work moves along in a direct line as it passes from the stock pile to the various machines and, finally, to the place

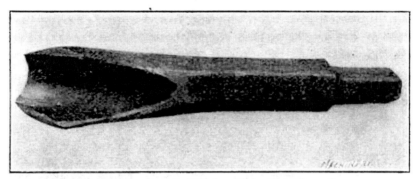

Fig. 16. Gouge-shaped Chisel used for Rounding Corners

where it is to be assembled. When we consider how many parts are incorporated in a single modern locomotive and then remember that approximately one such locomotive is being built daily at the Juniata shops, the importance of direct methods and their bearing on the rate of production can readily be appreciated.

Fig. 17. Frames after the Chipping is Completed

When the frames reach the erecting department, all corners are rounded by pneumatic hammers (as indicated in Fig. 15) before assembling. The chisels used for this work are shown in Fig. 16. They are shaped somewhat like a gouge but have a concave cutting edge. The corners are finished to the required radius by a single cut and almost as smoothly and neatly as could be done in a planer with a form tool. Two frames which have been finished in this way and are ready for the erecting gang, are shown in Fig. 17. This rounding of corners gives the frames a finished appearance and also makes it much easier to handle them, as all sharp edges have been cut away. It is also thought that a frame having round corners is less liable to fracture than one having square ragged corners, the theory being that a minute indentation at the corner may, in time, develop a fracture.

Fig. 18. Special Machine for Turning the Frame Bolts

The main frame and the trailer frame (in this particular case) are next aligned and the bolt holes for the splice at *A*, Fig. 4, are reamed. After the splice bolts are inserted, the right and left frame sections are tied together by the different cross-braces, and this is the first step in erecting a locomotive. The two sections are mounted on blocks and jacks and are then set level and parallel with each other. The various cross-ties and braces are temporarily clamped in position for reaming the previously drilled holes. As all the parts are accurately drilled, the holes are usually in close alignment, so that little reaming is necessary to produce a smooth hole which will insure an even bearing throughout the length of the bolt.

The reaming is done by means of an air motor, and the time required for reaming a hole and driving a bolt "home" is a matter of seconds rather than minutes. The reamer is entered into the hole and the motor-driven chuck is applied to the end. As the reamer only has a taper of 3/32 inch per foot (which is the standard for all frame bolts), it is quickly fed to the required depth. The reamer is then backed out while it rotates in the same direction, and the chips are blown from the hole by turning the air exhaust of the motor into it. A standard bolt is next inserted and driven home by a few blows of the sledge.

Fig. 19. Frame after Cylinders, Braces and other Parts
have been assembled

This entire operation of reaming the hole, cleaning it and driving in the bolt, is done in a surprisingly short time. As these men are constantly at this work, they have become very expert. No gages are required for reaming, as the workmen know just how far to feed in the reamer for any given bolt. When a hole is being reamed, the motor is held by two men, while a third man measures the distance between the reamer driving chuck and the frame in order to determine when the reamer has reached the required depth. When a reamer becomes too dull to work effectively, it is sharpened in a special grinding machine. The importance of keeping the reamers in good condition can best be appreciated by those who have tried to true up a hole with a dull reamer. Before the erection of the frames is complete, they must be bolted to the cylinder castings which form the principal support at the front. Fig. 19 shows an assembled frame after the cylinders, braces, guide-yoke and other parts connected with the spring and brake rigging, have been attached. When the work has reached this stage, it is only a matter of a few hours when the frame will be buried behind the driving wheels of the assembled locomotive.

Turning Frame Bolts

The method of turning the frame bolts used in assembling the frames is interesting, owing to the rapidity and simplicity of the operation. The machine used resembles an ordinary four-spindle drilling machine, as will be seen by referring to Fig. 18. The spindles are equipped with chucks having hexagonal pockets, not unlike a socket wrench, which fit the heads of the bolts and cause them to revolve while the body is being turned. The turning is done by cutter heads located in the base. There are two heads for roughing and a similar number for finishing. The roughing heads have two blades or cutters which are about 5/16 inch or 3/8 inch thick and 1¼ inch long. These cutters are set diametrically opposite, and they remove the hard outer scale. The bolt body is rough turned close to the finished size, but this first operation leaves it straight or of one diameter throughout. The work is then placed in a finishing head. These heads also contain two cutters which differ from those used in the roughing heads in that they are as long, or longer, than the bolt body and are set to turn the bolt body to the required taper. The turning operation, in each case, is performed by feeding the revolving bolt down through a cutter head just as a drill would be fed through its work. Several of these cutter heads may be seen at the base of the machine. They are mounted in floating holders so that they can adjust themselves to the bolt being turned. Very rapid work can be done in this machine, one man keeping the four heads in operation. The threading of the bolts is done in regular bolt-threading machines.

CHAPTER II

MACHINING LOCOMOTIVE CYLINDERS*

The cylinders of locomotives vary considerably in their general arrangement, and the exact method of machining them depends altogether on the type; but as the variations in practice are of minor importance, we shall deal with the subject in a general way instead of describing in detail the operations for each particular design. The various operations referred to represent the practice at the Juniata shops of the Pennsylvania Railroad, where all the passenger locomotives and many of the freight class used in this extensive system are built.

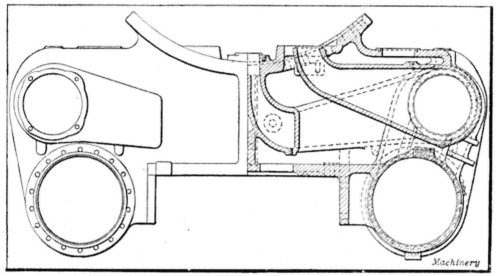

Fig. 20. Front View of Locomotive Cylinders of the Single-expansion
Piston Valve Type

The style of cylinder now used almost exclusively on the new locomotives built by the Pennsylvania Railroad is the single-expansion piston-valve type. Figs. 20 and 21 show two designs which differ in that the cylinders illustrated in Fig. 20 are cast integral with the saddle, whereas the cylinders shown in Fig. 21 are bolted to the saddle which forms a separate casting. The advantage of this three-piece construction is that a broken cylinder can be replaced more quickly because the saddle does not need to be detached from the boiler or frames. With the design shown in Fig. 20, considerable time is required to fit and bolt the flange on the saddle of a new cylinder to the boiler.

Boring the Cylinders

The first machining operation on a cylinder casting is that of boring the cylinder proper. The boring is done by the large machine illustrated in Figs. 22 and 24. The cylinder casting is supported at the

MACHINERY, Railway Edition, April, 1912.

right height by a fixture, as shown. The flanges are first rough-faced by radial facing arms *A* and *B*, the tools of which are fed by the well-known star feed. The bore is then finished by one roughing and one finishing cut, four tools being used for roughing and two for finishing. Broad-nosed tools are used for the light finishing cut and are given a feed of ⅜ inch per revolution of the boring-bar. As the boring-bar is very rigid, these coarse feeds can be used without chattering. The cylinder is also counterbored as far in as the inner edge of the steam ports, to prevent the piston-rings from wearing shoulders at the ends of the piston stroke.

After the cylinder bore is finished, the table or platen of the boring machine is moved over the right distance for boring the valve chamber,

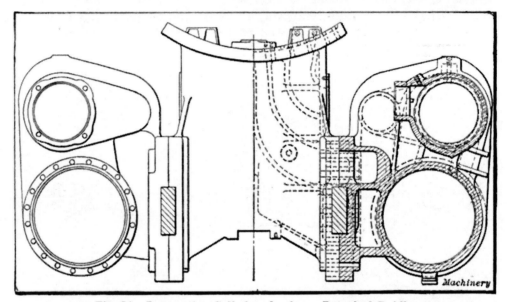

Fig. 21.   Locomotive Cylinders having a Detached Saddle

the proper adjustment being determined by graduation lines at the side of the table. In order that the valve chamber will be at the proper vertical height after making this adjustment, the casting is originally set up in the machine so that the centers of the cylinder and valve chamber are in the same horizontal plane. Fig. 24 shows the position of the work when set for boring the valve chamber. The flanges are faced prior to boring, and the offset of the flanges with relation to the cylinder flanges, is tested by a special gage. The valve chambers are not bored to one diameter throughout, but have a shoulder at each end for locating the valve bushings or linings which are afterward forced into the bore. The piston-valve operates inside these bushings, which can readily be renewed when worn. As the steam ports are machined in the bushings, the latter must be accurately located lengthwise to bring the ports in the right position. The proper location for each bushing is secured by the shoulder previously referred to, in conjunction with corresponding shoulders on the bushings; hence this shoulder in the bore must be accurately located by another special gage.

Planing the Cylinders

After the cylinder is bored, the various surfaces on the saddle are planed. By the use of an ingenious set of fixtures, the castings are quickly and accurately set up for the planing operations. Fig. 23 shows the cylinder planer with these fixtures in place, and Figs. 25, 26, and 28 show different views of the work mounted on the fixtures. Three cylinders are placed in a row and planed simultaneously, and the fixtures are so arranged that the bores of the various cylinders are aligned with one another and with the planer platen. These fixtures consist of heavy brackets or standards *B* having flanges as shown. The end brackets have a single flange, whereas the two which come between

Fig. 22. Boring a Locomotive Cylinder

the cylinders are double flanged. There is a central pocket *A* in each flange face, and the distance from these pockets to the base is exactly the same for each bracket. Each of the conical disks *C* which engage the counterbores of the cylinders, has a cylindrical boss *D* on the rear side which fits into any of the central pockets *A*. When a cylinder is to be set up for planing, one of these conical disks is clamped in each end of the counterbore by a bolt passing from one disk to the other. The brackets are also bolted to the planer platen in the proper position, as indicated in the illustration. The distance between the brackets is governed by the length between the outer faces of the disks after the latter are bolted in place, and the central pockets *A* are all brought into alignment, laterally, by tongue-pieces on the base of each bracket. The cylinder is next picked up by a crane and lowered until the disks have entered between the brackets. The temporary holding bolt for

Fig. 28. Fixture for Holding Cylinders while Planing

the disks is then removed and the work is lowered until the cylindrical bosses *D* on the disks, which slide through the vertical slots at *E*, rest in the central pockets *A* of the fixtures. When three cylinder castings have been set up in this way, the center line or axis of each cylinder bore will be in alignment.

The valve chamber is next set vertically with relation to the center of the cylinder. To obtain this setting, a spider *F*, Fig. 25, is placed in the valve chamber and its hub is centered with the bore of the valve chamber by using hermaphrodite calipers. The casting is then adjusted vertically by the small supporting jacks seen in Fig. 28, until this center is the required distance below the center of the cylinder, as shown by

Fig. 24. Cylinder set for Boring Valve Chamber

an ordinary surface gage. The height from the platen to the center of th cylinder bore is accurately ascertained beforehand and remains constant for a given size fixture. After the three castings are set as described, clamping pieces which fit in the slots *E*, Fig. 23, are tightened against the hubs of the conical disks by clamps *H*. The cylinders are further secured by a long tie-bolt *G*, Fig. 25, which extends through the three castings and holds both the work and fixtures rigidly together. The side view, Fig. 26, clearly shows how the conical disks enter the cylinder counterbores and align the three castings. By referring to Figs. 25 and 28, it will be seen that these fixtures make it possible to hold the three cylinders with very few clamps; in fact, the four clamps in Fig. 28 are (with the exception of clamps *H*, Fig. 23, which are part of the fixture) the only ones required. These fixtures have not only effected a considerable reduction in the time required for setting the

Fig. 26. Side View showing Arrangement of Planing Fixtures

Fig. 25. Three Cylinders being planed simultaneously

cylinders prior to planing, but they also insure accurate and uniform work.

After the cylinders are set as described, the top surface *I*, Fig. 25, which forms the joint between the right- and left-hand cylinders, is rough-planed by using the two tool-heads. This surface is then finished with a broad tool which is set to the right height for the final cut by a special micrometer gage *N*. The cutting edge is adjusted to coincide with the top of this gage, which is graduated with reference to the centers of the fixtures so that heights from the center of the cylinder bore can be read directly. The side *J* is next roughed out and finished

Fig. 27. Planing Cylinders of the "Three-piece" Type

by using a side-head, and while this surface is being planed, the seats *K* and *L* (Fig. 28) for the steam and exhaust pipes, are rough-planed with the opposite side-head. Side *J* is finished to a certain distance from the planer housing, the measurement being taken with a special vernier gage. By measuring directly from the housing, duplicate work is assured and the liability of mistakes is lessened. This method of measuring is made practicable by the improved fixtures, which are always located in the same lateral position on the platen and, consequently, hold the finished cylinder bores in the same vertical and crosswise position. The face *M*, against which the frame is bolted subsequently, is planed at the same time the seats *K* and *L* are finished. The half-seat *K* for the exhaust pipe, is gaged from the finished side *J* and the steam pipe seat *L* is finished with reference to the exhaust seat. The distance between surfaces *I* and *M* is measured by a special height gage. This practically completes the planer work. Of course, the order

Fig. 28. General View of Cylinder Planer—Note Small Number of Clamps used for Holding Work

of the operations is governed entirely by the shape of the cylinder casting, and differs from that described in the foregoing, for other types of cylinders.

Figs. 27 and 29 indicate the method of planing cylinders of the type illustrated in Fig. 21, which, as will be recalled, are bolted to the saddle. These castings are set up in the same way as described for the style illustrated in Fig. 28. The planer work on the cylinder proper is more easily done owing to the shape of the casting. The illustrations shows the two cross-rail heads rough-planing the saddle joint, while the left side-head is planing small pads on the steam chest. The

Fig. 29. Another View of the "Three-piece" Cylinders set up for Planing

tool is set for finishing the saddle joint by the same micrometer gage previously referred to, but a shorter measuring rod is inserted in the base for this particular style of cylinder. The pocket in the center of the saddle joint is finished to fit the frame, and in the right relation to the cylinder bore. There are also corresponding pockets in each side of the saddle casting, and the frames pass through the rectangular opening or mortises thus formed, as indicated by the section lines in Fig. 21. The planing of this saddle joint and pocket is practically all the planer work there is on a cylinder of this type. The nature of the planing operations on the saddle is clearly indicated by the drawing Fig. 21.

Laying Out and Drilling the Cylinders

After the cylinders are planed, the accuracy of the machine work previously done is tested and the casting is laid out for drilling holes that cannot conveniently be jig-drilled. Fig. 30 shows the method of

Fig. 31. Another View of Cylinder on Testing and Laying-out Plate

Fig. 30. Testing Height of Cylinder and Valve Chamber

testing the location of the cylinder bore and valve chamber with relation to each other and to the finished central joint which is resting
on the laying-out plate. The centering spiders shown are first accurately set in each bore and the respective heights of the cylinder and
valve chamber are determined by using a tall surface gage. These
heights are measured by comparing the gage pointer with a long steel

Fig. 32. Drilling Frame Bolt Holes

scale held in a vertical position. While the use of the planing fixtures
previously described insures accurate work, it has been found advisable to check important dimensions so that the cylinders can be
erected without delay due to imperfect work. After the height of each
bore has been checked, as described, the distance from the face of the
back cylinder flange to the finished projection *A* is carefully tested, as
this projecting flange rests against the frame and determines the cylinder's fore-and-aft location.

Most of the holes in the cylinder are, of course, drilled by the use of jigs. There are, however, a few holes which cannot conveniently be drilled in this way and these are laid out at this time. For example, the small screw holes around the periphery of the flange, for fastening the cylinder jacket, as well as those for lubricator and indicator pipes, dripcocks, etc., are all laid out by hand. A center line *L* (see Fig 34) is also drawn across the saddle face for locating the jig used when

Fig. 33. Drilling Flanges

drilling the bolt holes for the steam and exhaust pipe seats at *S* and *E*. This line is exactly central with the front and back flange faces of the cylinder. A central point is first located at L_1, Fig. 31, by measuring from a long straightedge held across the front and back flanges. The cylinder is then turned over and this line is carried across the saddle joint by using a large square.

The drilling operations on the cylinder are of an obvious nature and therefore a detailed description of this work will be unnecessary. Prac-

tically all the holes are drilled by the use of jigs in large radial machines. Fig. 32 shows a plate jig for drilling the frame bolt holes.
This jig is located by the finished end *A* on the cylinder, and the jig
for drilling the corresponding holes in the frame is set by a shoulder
which bears against end *A*, so that both sets of holes register closely
when the cylinder and frame are assembled; consequently, little reaming is necessary. The holes for the stud bolts which hold the cylinder
and the steam chest heads in place, are drilled with ordinary ring jigs
as indicated in Fig. 33. Fig. 34 shows the method of forming the seat
for the steam pipe. This pipe is not clamped directly to the cylinder,

Fig. 34. Reaming Seat for Steam Pipe

but bears against a cast-iron ring having a flat face on one side and
a spherical face on the other. The large reamer *R* forms this spherical
seat, which is clearly shown in the view to the left, Fig. 35.

Erecting Cylinders—Piston-valve Bushings

When the drilling is completed the cylinders are ready for the erecting shop. The right- and left-hand cylinders which are to be mates,
are set up and aligned as illustrated in the two views Fig. 35. The
saddle bolts through the front and rear flanges *F* are then reamed and
the tightly fitting taper bolts are inserted. The cylinders are now ready
to be attached to the frames. They are first bolted to the frames temporarily, and their position is carefully tested. The bolt holes are next
reamed and the right and left frame sections are bolted to their respective cylinders.

The bushings or linings for the valve chambers are also inserted at this time.   There are two of these bushings in each cylinder, which are inserted from opposite ends of the valve chamber bore.   The inside of the bushing is bored to fit the piston-valve, and the outside is turned to fit tightly into the cylinder.   The boring is done in a vertical boring machine, and the outside is turned in a lathe (as indicated in Fig. 36), after the boring operation.   The bushing is mounted on a large expanding mandrel, and it is turned from 0.002 to 0.004 inch larger than the bore of the valve chamber, in order to secure a tight fit.   This allowance varies somewhat for bushings of different diameter.   After the bushing is turned, the steam and exhaust ports, which are cored in the

Fig. 35.   Cylinders aligned for Reaming Flange Bolt Holes

casting, are finished by milling.   Two finished bushings are shown to the right in Fig. 36.   The large ports *E* are for the exhaust and the smaller ports *S* register with the cylinder steam ports when the bushings are in place.   These ports are milled to a standard width by the use of gages.   They are also located with reference to the shoulders *L* which, as previously stated, come against corresponding shoulders in the valve chamber, and determine the respective positions of the bushings.   The distance between the steam ports is checked before the bushings are inserted in the cylinder.   This preliminary test is made by placing the two bushings in line, with the shoulders *L* the same distance apart as the shoulders in the valve chamber.   The distance between the inner edges of the steam ports is then measured with a large vernier scale *V*.   A variation of only 0.004 inch is allowed for this dimension.   As the distance between the packing rings of the piston-valves, and also the width of the rings, is accurately gaged, the proper relation between the valve and the steam ports is secured within close limits.

The finished bushings are drawn into the valve chamber by a screw and air motor as shown in Fig. 37. This particular illustration shows the motor arranged for drawing in the rear bushing. The screw, which is rotated by the motor, is prevented from moving longitudinally by a heavy strap which is placed across the flange as shown. After both bushings are drawn in against the shoulders, the distance between the steam ports is again tested with the vernier scale. This second meas-

Fig. 36. Method of Turning Valve Bushings and Preliminary Test to determine Location of Steam Ports

urement is taken to make sure that the bushings are not held away from their seats by small chips or dirt which may have been overlooked when the bore was cleaned. Before the boiler can be erected, the curved seat or saddle formed by the two cylinders must be fitted to the front of the smokebox. As the steel sheet which forms the smokebox may not be exactly circular, the saddle is always fitted to the particular boiler for which it is intended. In order to obtain the required outline, the boiler is lowered by a crane onto the frames and cylinders. The boiler is then set level, both lengthwise and laterally, and it is also centered with the frames. The outline of the smokebox is then transferred to the saddle flanges, by using a scratch gage. This line represents the finished surface of the saddle, and it should be drawn just far enough from the top surface, to permit truing the entire saddle flange. When this line is scribed, the boiler is removed and a gang of men chip the flange down to the required outline. This chipping is done by pneumatic hammers. There are raised pads on the saddle flange as shown in the view to the left, Fig. 35, so that a comparatively small surface requires chipping. When the flange is finished, the boiler

Fig. 37. Drawing in Valve Bushing with Air Motor

is permanently bolted to the cylinders, and when this stage is reached, the erection of the locomotive proceeds rapidly. The erecting practice is described in MACHINERY's Reference Book No. 84, "Locomotive Building, Part VI."

MACHINERY'S REFERENCE SERIES

EACH NUMBER IS ONE UNIT IN A COMPLETE LIBRARY OF
MACHINE DESIGN AND SHOP PRACTICE REVISED AND
REPUBLISHED FROM MACHINERY

NUMBER 82

LOCOMOTIVE BUILDING

By Ralph E. Flanders

PART IV

VALVE MOTION—TOOL-ROOM PRACTICE

CONTENTS

Copyright, 1912, The Industrial Press, Publishers of MACHINERY
49-55 Lafayette Street, New York City.

CHAPTER I

MAKING WALSCHAERTS VALVE GEAR*

Every mechanic really interested in mechanics, who chances to live near one of the great trunk line railroads, must have noticed a remarkable change in locomotive design which has taken place in the last four or five years. We refer to the increasing use of the Walschaerts valve gear. A locomotive equipped with this gear, as shown in Fig. 1, presents a distinctly different appearance from one furnished with the old-style Stephenson link motion, which is mounted out of sight between the frames of the engine. This difference in appearance is especially noticeable with the engine running at high speed when the lines of flashing light made by the flying steel work of the rods and links give a decidedly mazy and complicated appearance to the mechanism.

The Advantages of the Walschaerts Gear

In reality, however, the Walschaerts gear is not as complicated as the Stephenson type. The deciding factor in its adoption, as every railroad man knows, was not the matter of complication, but of dimensions. Of late years engines have grown so tremendously in size and power that it has become next to impossible to find room between the frames for eccentrics and valve movements of sufficient size and wearing area to give strength and durability for the heavy service required of them. Besides this, the large diameter of the axles of heavy locomotives requires an eccentric of correspondingly large diameter; and with this, the surface speed of the bearing of the eccentric strap on the eccentric is so great as to practically nullify the effect of any increased area which could be given to it by careful designing. These considerations led to the adoption of a form of valve gear which was located entirely outside the wheels, where no serious dimensional limitations were placed on the parts.

When it came to the actual application of the new motion to the locomotive, it was found to have further advantages. One of them lay in the fact that it is always exposed to the view, making it very easy to erect and maintain, leaving it open for the constant inspection of the engineer. Besides this, it may be easily so designed that all its movements are in straight lines, without canting or side strains, thus practically adapting it to heavy service. In the matter of steam distribution and economy, there is little to choose between the two, though the old gear may have a slight advantage.

We have referred to the Walschaerts gear as a "new" form of gear. This is true, however, only for American service. It has been used

*MACHINERY, June, 1910.

Fig. 1. Pennsylvania R. R. Pacific Type Passenger Locomotive with Form of Walschaerts Valve Gear used for Heavy Service

to a limited extent in England, but on the Continent it has been employed almost to the exclusion of any other form of valve gear ever since its invention by a Belgian, Egide Walschaerts, about 1844. Although we were so slow in adopting it in this country, its good qualities were rapidly recognized when once the start was made, as is evidenced by the fact that of 2448 locomotives ordered in this country in 1909, 1638, or about 67 per cent, were of the Walschaerts type; 30 per cent were of the Stephenson type; while the remaining 3 per cent of the total number were furnished with other designs of valve movements, some of which were of a more or less experimental nature.

Two Designs of the Walschaerts Gear

The first two illustrations show the mechanism as applied to the locomotive. Different designs are shown in the two cases, that in Fig. 1 being used for the heavy service, while that in Fig. 2 is adapted to lighter work, being applied in this case to the standard Atlantic type passenger locomotive of the Pennsylvania R. R. The main dif-

Fig. 2. Design of Walschaerts Valve Gear used on Atlantic Type Engines

ference relates to the method of raising and lowering the radius rod in the link, the connection between the radius rod and the link block, and the support of the link.

In Fig. 1 the link is mounted on swinging yokes on each side, pivoted to bearings on a cast-steel frame. The radius rod is provided with an extension, which spans the link on each side inside of the yokes and is provided with a finished square shank projecting beyond the link, which bears in the pivoted block on the end of the reversing arm, by which it is raised and lowered for forward and backward running. In Fig. 2 the link is supported in trunnions or saddles at the center, and the radius rod is hung from the reversing arm on a short link.

The operations on the rod work of the valve mechanism in the Juniata shops do not differ materially, except that the work is smaller, from the method of manufacture used in making the main and side rods, described in MACHINERY's Reference Book No. 79, "Locomotive Building, Part I, Main and Side Rods." In describing the shop operations on this valve gear, we will, therefore, confine the description to two particular parts of a special and peculiar design—namely,

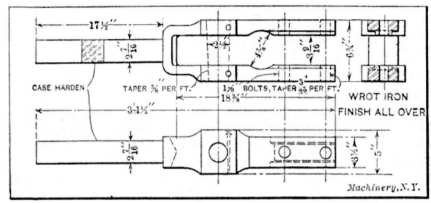

Fig. 3. Radius Rod Extension for Valve Gear shown in Fig. 1

the links for both types of valve gear, and the radius rod extension for the heavier type of locomotive shown in Fig. 1.

Roughing Out the Radius Rod Extension

A drawing of the radius rod extension is shown in Fig. 3. As may be seen, it is made from a wrought-iron forging, and is finished all

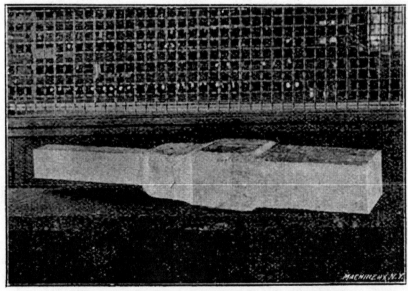

Fig. 4. Rough Forging for Radius Rod Extension

over. The square projecting shank, which bears in the pivoted block of the reversing arm is casehardened to give a durable wearing surface. This casehardening, as will be explained, introduced some difficulties in the course of manufacture. The overcoming of these difficulties gives the part its particular interest from the machinist's standpoint.

The rough forging from which the piece is made is shown in Fig. 4. The illustration shows that the ends of this forging have been trimmed to size in the cold saw to practically the required length for the finished piece. Fig. 5 shows this forging roughed out all over. The various cuts shown have been taken in the slotting machine and the shaper. On the shank, which is to be casehardened, the rough stock

Fig. 5. Forging Roughed all over and Shank Finished

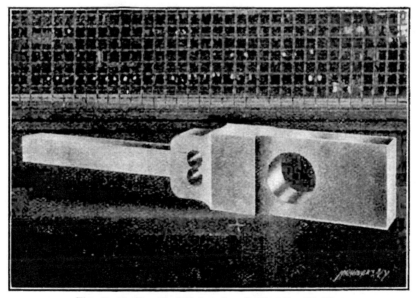

Fig. 6. Radius Rod Extension Drilled for Slotting

was in the first place necked out close to the connection with the body of the forging, the cuts being taken crosswise of the work on the four sides, on the slotter. The forging was then taken to the shaper and the square was finished down to size. This, of course, is the obvious method of procedure.

The holes have next to be drilled for slotting out the interior of the blank to form the two arms which encircle the link. The machining of these holes is performed on a heavy drill press; or, as in the case shown at the left of Fig. 7, on a regular rod boring machine, using only one of the spindles. leaving the other free for other work. The larger hole is first drilled out, and then it is bored with a bar carrying a double-edged blade, as shown in the engraving. After these boring and drilling operations, the work has arrived at the stage shown in Fig. 6.

Fig. 7. Drilling Radius Rod Extension and Walschaerts Links

The forging is now taken to the slotting machine, where (see Fig. 8) it is mounted on parallels, so as to hold it firmly and accurately to the table of the machine. A square-nosed tool is used for cutting out the block of stock between the holes. The C-clamp, which is shown tightened in place on the forging, prevents the two sides of the newly formed opening from separating under the pressure of the cut. The state of the work at the end of this operation is shown in Fig. 9.

Casehardening the Shanks of the Radius Rod Extension

It has been found advisable to caseharden the shank at this point in the procedure. The advantage of doing it at this time lies in the fact that the remainder of the work is not yet finished to its final dimensions and the two sides are still tied together by the mass of material left between them at the outer end. Thus the distortion which is sure to take place in work of this kind in hardening, takes place at a time when it does no harm, as the finishing cuts will be taken with reference to the finished and casehardened surfaces of the shank, with which they will, therefore, be true and accurate. If the opening between the two sides were completely cut out, as shown

Fig. 8. Working out the Slot in the Slotting Machine

Fig. 9. Work with Center Slotted out ready for Casehardening

in Fig. 3, before this hardening operation, they would almost certainly be sprung out of parallel with each other, or out of line with the casehardened portion.

Fig. 10 shows the casehardening furnace and two pieces of work ready for heating. The furnace is fired with oil, and supplied by a blast from the regular blower service of the forge shop. Provision is made, however, for an independent blast for keeping up the fire

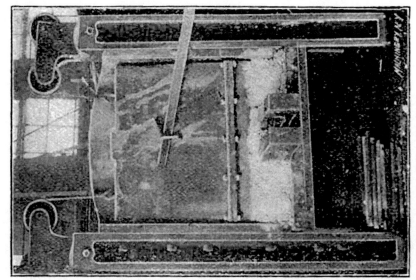

Fig. 12. Casehardening Furnace ready for the Heating

Fig. 11. Work Placed in Furnace ready for Casehardening

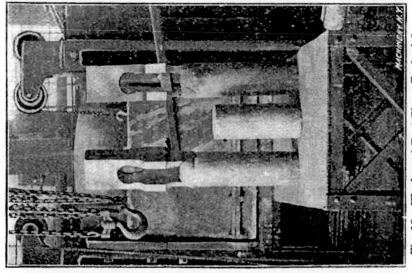

Fig. 10. Work and Test Piece Packed for Hardening

during the night or at times when the regular forge service is not in operation. This independent service is furnished by a small blower fan, which is itself operated by impingement on its blades of a jet of air from the high-pressure shop service line, used for the pneumatic hammers, riveters, etc. This latter is kept continually under pressure, day and night, so it is available any hour of the twenty-four, making it possible to use the furnace at any time or for any length of time.

As may be seen in Fig. 10, only that portion of the work which is to be hardened is packed. This is inserted in a section of wrought iron pipe, filled with the casehardening material, composed of 11 pounds of prussiate of potash, 30 pounds of sal-soda, 20 pounds of coarse salt and 6 bushels of powdered charcoal (hickory-wood charcoal preferred), thoroughly mixed with 30 quarts of water. The pipe is luted with

Fig. 13. Cooling the Casehardened Shank of the Work.

fire-clay at each end to retain the carbonizing material and exclude the air. The work is placed in the furnace as shown in Figs. 11 and 12. The part that is not to be made hard is left projecting outside the furnace door. A wall of fire-brick and clay is built up to close the space between the lower edge of the door and the bottom of the furnace opening. After soaking for, say, fourteen hours, more or less, the work is removed from the furnace and from its packing, and plunged into a tank of water as shown in Fig. 13, being suspended there until cool.

Test Pieces for Casehardening

Fig. 13 also shows a square block of hammered iron marked "Test piece." The use of this test piece gives an idea of the precautions which the Pennsylvania officials have found it wise to adopt to make sure that all the material and treatment given to the vital parts of their locomotives, are up to the standard required of them. This test piece is forged at the same time and from the same material as the radius rod extensions. It is machined to the same dimensions as the square shank of the extension which is to be casehardened. It is packed in a similar wrought-iron casing, as shown between the two pieces of work in Fig. 10, and is placed in the casehardening furnace next to the work itself, remaining there for the same time and subjected to the same degree of heat. It is then cooled and hardened in the same manner. It is evident, then, that the condition of the test

Fig. 14. Broken Test Pieces for Showing Condition of the Work.

Fig. 15. End View of the Test Pieces showing Depth of Hardened
Portion and Character of Fracture

piece should give an accurate index of the condition of the work itself, so far as the hardening operation is concerned.

The test piece, thus prepared, is now taken to a press and broken, in order that the condition of the interior may be noted. Figs. 14 and 15 show various examples of these broken test pieces. The examination shows the condition of the metal, the texture of the fiber, and the depth of the casehardening. One-half of each test piece is thrown away. The other half is retained, marked with the date of hardening and the class and construction number of the engine on which the casehardened parts are to be used. These are kept two years, until it is proved that the work is giving good service, and it is certain that no trouble is to be expected from it. It is held by the shop as a sort of guarantee of the good work done in the heat treatment.

Such precautions would hardly be necessary or advisable in any other kind of work, but there are many cases in locomotive practice where the extra expense and trouble is worth while. A defect in a

Fig. 16. Charcoal Crusher Built on the Bone Mill Principle

locomotive is a serious matter. It may mean nothing worse than the delay of thousands of tons of valuable freight, or it may mean the loss of human life and serious damage to the prestige of a great railway system. Good steel properly treated is absolutely essential for the vital parts of a locomotive, and every precaution is taken to insure reliability.

It was mentioned that ground charcoal is one of the ingredients used in casehardening. Fig. 16 shows the mill used here for grinding the charcoal. It had formerly been broken by workmen with hammers. in much the same primitive fashion that ice is pounded for the ice-cream freezer in the ordinary American home. The foreman discarded this primitive process, however, and bethought himself of a bone grinding mill used on a chicken ranch in his neighborhood, which he proceeded to copy. His copy is made of a few simple castings, and consists essentially of a hopper, as shown, having projections on the inside, alternating with similar projections on a revolving cone. The inner surface of the conical hopper and revolving cone taper toward each other, and as the charcoal passes through the revolving teeth into this narrowing space, it is crushed finer and finer until it drops through a spout into the box. The fineness can be regulated by raising and lowering the hopper by means of the adjusting nuts on the studs by which it is supported. This crusher is operated by an air motor.

Finishing Operations on the Radius Rod Extension

Fig. 17 shows the completed radius rod and extension assembled. The remaining machining operations have been performed, as required by Fig. 3, finishing out the slot between the two sides of the fork, and machining them for the tongue and groove joint of the radius rod head. These tongues are made with a taper, as shown, so that they bear on the sides only. When the bolts are tightened down to form the joint, assurance is given of a firm grip with no possibility of play or backlash.

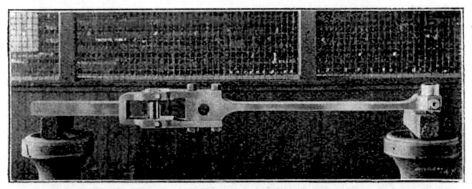

Fig. 17. Radius Rod Extension with Slotting Complete—Assembled with Radius Rod

Another point should be noticed in Fig. 3, which is a regular practice in locomotive construction, but one with which many machine-tool machinists are unfamiliar. This practice is the use of taper bolts. The two bolts shown, which hold the joint, are of 1¼ inch normal diameter, but they are tapered on the body of the bolt 3/32 inch per foot. This is the standard practice for all important bolts used throughout the whole locomotive. After the holes are drilled, the taper reamer is run through them to such a depth that, when the bolts are screwed home, they will draw in to a tight fit in the holes, and come solidly against the head. Each bolt thus serves as a well-fitted dowel, in addition to its duty of drawing the parts together. When the work is properly made, the joint thus formed is of a superior character.

Roughing Out the Link

A general drawing of the link used for the heavy form of Walschaerts gear is shown in Fig. 18. As was explained in connection with Fig. 1, this is of the kind in which the link is supported by yokes which are attached to it at each end of the slot, and are provided with central pivots mounted in stationary bearings in the side frames. The two jaws of the radius rod span the link inside of the yokes in a way that will be understood by comparing Figs. 1, 17 and 18. The

Fig. 19. Planing the Forging for Links

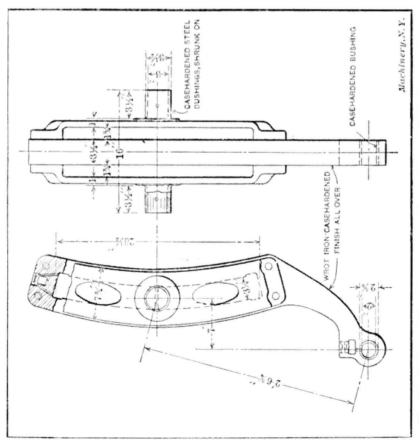

Machinery, N.Y.

Fig. 18. Link and Mounting used for Heavy Type of Walschaerts Gear

method of manufacture to be described applies in general to the light form of link shown in Fig. 2 as well as to the heavier type.

The first operation is the simple one of machining the sides of the rough forging from which the link is made. This is done in the planer with the usual holding devices as shown in Fig. 19. In Fig. 20 these forgings, which have been finished on each side to the required thickness, are laid out on horses, for marking off with a templet. The further one has the templet clamped to it as shown. From this the outline of the finished piece is scribed, together with the outline of the curved slot for the link block. The location of the pivot for the return crank rod is also indicated, as well as that of the four holes for holding on the yokes. This is an example of

Fig. 20. Laying out the Links with Sheet-iron Templet

standard practice in this shop, where the use of an inexpensive templet saves a great deal of time in laying out work, and gives assurance of proper location of the various machining cuts.

The slot has next to be worked out. As indicated in Fig. 7, the forgings are first drilled through at the ends and in the middle of the slot, one end of the rod boring machine being conveniently employed for the purpose when not otherwise engaged. The links are then taken to the slotting machine, where the stock is roughly worked out by a parting tool as shown in Fig. 21. Two forgings are operated on at a time, with the holes lined up with each other. The parting tool is fed from one hole to the other on each side, removing thin slices of metal from the interior of the slot, and leaving it in condition for finishing to size.

Finishing the Slot of the Link

This finishing operation is performed on a link planing attachment of the usual construction, shown in use in Fig. 22. It would not be necessary to explain this device to railroad men, but for non-railroad readers the accompanying sketch, Fig. 23, will explain the principle.

The link, shown at *A*, is mounted on a table *B* with T-slots on the top, which swivels about pin *C* fast in the base *D*. The swiveling of this table is governed by a stud *E* having a roller engaging a swivel guide *F*, clamped to the under side of the ram, or traveling head of the shaper. By setting the guide *F* to the proper angle, it so swivels the work about pivot *C* that the tool *G* will cut to a line closely approximating the true arc of a circle.

Fig. 21. Slotting the Links Two at a Time after Drilling as in Fig. 7

Fig. 22. Planing the Slots in the Links with Link Planing Attachment

The diagram Fig. 23 shows the mechanism as applied to the planer rather than to the open-side shaper, inasmuch as it shows guide *F* and tool-point *G* stationary, while the work *A* and work-table *B* are moving backward and forward. The principle is, of course, the same as in Fig. 22, except that here the work-table *B* (Fig. 23) is stationary and the guide *F* reciprocates with tool *G*, swiveling table *B* and work *A* about stationary pivot *C*. It should be noted that whenever the tool is changed in this attachment for any reason, it must always be set up again with dimension *X* (the distance from the tool-point to the center of the swivel of guide *F*) always the same. If this distance is altered, the radius and position of the arc are changed.

Inasmuch as the surfaces of the link, thus finished, are approximate and not exactly true, it is customary to finish them more nearly to absolute truth. This is done by grinding on the radius grinder to a good bearing for the templet shown in Fig. 24, which is itself

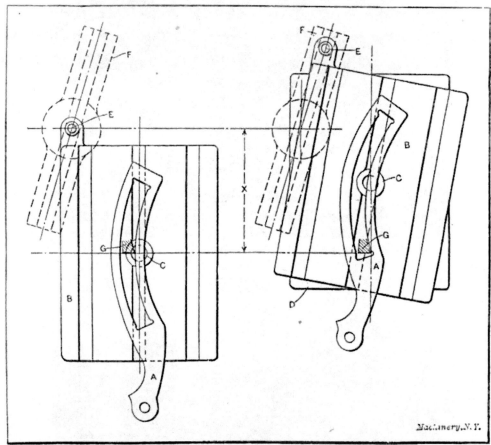

Fig. 23. Principle of Radius Link Planing Attachment for the Planer

accurately machined to the proper radius, and to the proper thickness. It should have been mentioned that the pockets at the ends of the slot have been cut out in a succeeding slotting machine operation to that shown in Fig. 21. These pockets give room for the shaper tool to run out into, as in Fig. 23.

Drilling and Finishing the Link

The slot in the link being the important surface, succeeding operations of importance are located from it. The next thing to be done is the drilling of the holes for the connection with the return crank rod. This operation, which is not shown here, is performed by means of a simple jig, located by a templet fitting the link slot, and carrying a bushing in the proper position for the hole.

The outline of the link has next to be finished. This is done as shown in Fig. 25 in a vertical milling machine, the table being rotated and fed by hand or power as required, following the outline scribed by the templet. Two links at a time are machined in this way, taking up nearly the full width of the cutter shown in use. They are lined

Fig. 24. Templet used for Finishing the Slot in the Link for the Radius Rod

Fig. 25. Outlining the Links on the Vertical Milling Machine

up with each other by a pin through the return crank rod connection hole, and by lining up the sides of the slots.

The oil holes have next to be drilled, and the bolt holes for attaching the yokes. In the case of Fig. 18, the bolt holes are drilled in a way similar to that employed for drilling the return rod connection —namely, by means of a jig carrying a templet which fits the slot, and is provided with a bushing set at the proper relation to the templet. The yokes themselves, shown in place in Fig. 27, are drilled by a jig which is located from the pivots on which the yokes swing. The holes for holding together the yokes and link are thus so located that the pivots are in the proper position with relation to the slot, and thus are in line with each other as well. These positions and the location of the holes for the return crank rod being the important dimensions, are all located from the slot of each link, and so are in the proper relation to each other.

Fig. 26 shows the method of locating the saddles or pivot supports used for the link on the light type of valve gear shown in Fig. 2. Here a fixture *J* is set into the link slot which fits it snugly, and is provided with pockets for receiving the saddles *H*, which are thus

Fig. 26. Jig used for Locating Pivot Saddles on Atlantic Type Link

accurately located from the journals of the pivots. When thus located, each is held in place by a set-screw as shown.. The whole attachment is now slid along through the slot until it makes contact with the distance piece *K*, which is mounted on a stud fitted in the return crank rod hole. By this means, the pivots are located as they should be, with proper reference to the slot, and with proper reference to the return rod connection.

After the yokes in Fig. 27 and the saddles in Fig. 26 have been drilled and bolted into place, the outlines of these members are finished off to match evenly with the outlines of the link, making a good smooth job. Figs. 27 and 28 show a completed link of the heavy type, with the block in place ready for assembling in the locomotive.

Manufacturing Methods in Locomotive Building

Locomotives are built at Altoona on a manufacturing basis. When we make this statement, the words "manufacturing basis" mean something different than they do when we say that typewriters or machine tools are so built. In fact the term has a different meaning for all three cases. Manufacturing methods in building locomotives do not involve the use of jigs and fixtures for finishing all the massive parts of which the great machine is built. Jigs and fixtures large enough

Fig. 27. Complete Pacific Type Link with Yokes in Place

Fig. 28. Another View of the Finished Pacific Type Link

to do this would be prohibitive in size and cost, and practically no advantage would be gained from their use in any event.

The "manufacturing basis" on which the locomotive is built involves the use of templets for laying off all important outlines, holes, etc. Comparatively few holes are drilled in jigs, those so drilled being mostly the ones on which the accuracy of the valve gear lay-out depends, such as the radius rod and yoke connections in the link we have just described. In locomotive manufacture large use is also made of fixed gages for all the vital measurements of the frame, axles, etc., and for such other parts as are likely to require renewal. These parts are thus practically made on the interchangeable plan, though no such extreme of refinement is needed as that necessary in making typewriter parts interchangeable.

It will be seen that the tools required for this manufacturing work are of the simplest possible nature. The templets are made of sheet iron; the gages are made from bar steel, drawn down and ground at the points to the proper dimensions; and the fixtures are, in general, of a rugged and simple construction. By following this plan, the expense for tools is of comparatively small importance, even when building only two or three locomotives of a kind. At the same time advantage is taken of about all the benefits of accuracy and interchangeability which can be secured on such large work.

The New K-2 Pacific Type Locomotive

It may be interesting to give a few particulars of the locomotive shown in Fig. 1. This is, as may be seen, of the Pacific type, which has come to be a standard machine for hauling the heavier high-speed passenger trains. The Pennsylvania R. R. has hitherto been able to maintain the schedules on its passenger runs with locomotives of the Atlantic type (see Fig. 2) of considerable lighter weight than other roads had found necessary for the same purpose. It was decided, however, a short time ago, to experiment with heavier machines, and the K-2 locomotive shown herewith is the result. This is probably the heaviest passenger locomotive ever built, outside of the Mallet articulated machines furnished to the Santa Fe, which are in a class by themselves.

The total weight of the engine alone is 270,000 pounds, of which 176,500 pounds are on the driving wheels. The wheels are 80 inches in diameter. A straight boiler is used 80 inches in diameter at the front end. The grate area is 61.8 square feet. The total heating surface is 4427 square feet. The cylinders are 24 inches in diameter with a 26-inch stroke. The total cylinder horsepower developed is something over 2000, giving about 134 pounds weight per horsepower for engine and boiler. Comparison with any figures which might be taken from stationary practice of similar size would show a tremendously higher ratio than this, giving a good idea of the high degree of specialization which has been reached in locomotive design.

The diameters of the wheels and boiler are so large that even the liberal clearance allowed by the Pennsylvania R. R. have necessitated the shortening of the stack and domes to an unusual degree.

CHAPTER II

SPECIAL TOOL-ROOM APPLIANCES*

The tool-room at the Juniata Shops of the Pennsylvania Railroad, at Altoona, Pa., is remarkable for the range in size and accuracy of the work it is called upon to perform. Not only do they make here the rough dies required for bull-dozer and other machine forging operations, but the workmen are prepared at a moment's notice to break off on such work and undertake the building of the fine instrument parts for a locomotive test plant or a precision dynamometer car. Besides this ability to do fine work, there is a large fund of

Fig. 29. Micrometer for Measuring Odd-fluted Reamers, etc.

ingenuity in the organization. The tools and devices herewith illustrated and described will give ample evidence of the truth of this assertion.

Micrometer for Odd-fluted Reamers

Fig. 29 shows a simple special micrometer. It is used for measuring the diameters of counterbores, reamers, etc., with odd numbers of flutes. It performs this awkward operation in a simple and easy manner. As may be seen, the instrument resembles a vernier caliper, having a blade provided with a split hub for clamping to the tail center of the grinding machine; the usual adjustable jaw and fine adjustment slides are provided. There are, however, no scale or vernier graduations. What would ordinarily be the jaw carries a micrometer spindle instead.

*MACHINERY, September, 1910.

To illustrate the use of this instrument, suppose it is desired to grind a counterbore, like that shown, to a diameter of 2.396 inches. First a standard 2-inch plug gage is set on the centers of the grinder, and the slide or jaw carrying the micrometer spindle is adjusted until the graduations on the spindle read to zero when the point of the measuring screw is brought down against the surface of the plug. The micrometer spindle is now screwed back out of the way, and the work is set in place on the centers. The counterbore is to be ground to a diameter 0.396 inch larger than that of the standard plug, or to a radius one-half that, or 0.198 inch, larger. It is therefore ground until, when measured by the micrometer in the way shown in the engraving, the graduations on the barrel of the micrometer

Fig. 30. Eccentric Grinding Device, for Straight and Taper Reamers

read 0.198 inch, which shows that the counterbore has been reduced to the required diameter.

Grinding Reamers with Eccentric Relief

Figs 30 and 31 show an eccentric reamer grinding device, which is in almost constant use, owing to the immense number of straight and (particularly) taper reamers used about a railroad shop. This device grinds the reamers eccentrically, so that they are provided with a better relief at the top of the blades than is given with the old-fashioned straight or concave grinding. The action consists in rocking the reamer about a center, so set as to give the proper contour to the blade being ground. This rocking takes place rapidly and continuously, while the table is moving the reamer back and forth past the wheel by the regular reversing feed mechanism.

The device is operated by a belt from the countershaft, running over the pulley which is mounted on a shaft connecting the two heads *C*. The mechanism is identical in each head. The shaft on which the pulley is mounted is connected by an adjustable cam movement with the sleeves *B* in which the work centers are mounted. This mechanism rocks the sleeves rapidly, and with them the work. The centers of each head may be adjusted in their sleeves to the proper degree of eccentricity and to the proper position. Provision is likewise made for indexing the reamer from one tooth to the other, as each is completed. As shown in Fig. 31, this consists of a gage *D*, provided with a tooth-rest against which each blade of the reamer is lined up in turn, while it is being adjusted for sharpening. This rest is swung out of the way before the rocking mechanism of the attachment is started.

All the various adjustments provided facilitate the operation of the grinding to such an extent that the device is practically as rapid in operation as the old style arrangement giving flat or concave relief; and at the same time it gives far superior results. The heads *C* can, of

Fig. 31. Rear View of Reamer Grinding Attachment, showing Tooth Gage

course, be set to any center distance, and the table of the machine can be set to any angle for taper reamers. All the other adjustable features of the standard grinding machine have also been retained.

The Thread Pitch Testing Machine

In Fig. 32 is shown what is in some respects the most interesting of the special tools which have been made and used at this shop. This is a thread testing device, which finds steady and profitable employment in the measurement of taps, stay-bolts, lead-screws, etc. The device is mounted on a baseplate *E*, and is provided with head- and foot-stocks *F* in which centered work is mounted, and with V-supports *G* for uncentered work. These are shown in use in Fig. 34. The V-supports are provided with vertical adjustments for bringing the center line of the work parallel with the base, and at the same height as the measuring points of the instrument.

The instrument or indicator itself is most plainly shown in the detail view in Fig. 33. It comprises a standard on which is pivoted a sensitive spring pointer *H*, and a stationary pointer *J*. The latter is mounted on a bar *K*, which may be minutely adjusted lengthwise by the adjusting screw *L*. The indications of pointer *H* are read on dial *M*, whose support may be adjusted in a circular dove-tailed slot about the center of the pivot of *H*, to bring the reading to zero whenever desired. This adjustment is effected by screw *N*, and is clamped

Fig. 32. Instrument for Testing the Accuracy of the Pitch of Screw Threads

Fig. 33. Detail View of the Thread Indicator

by screw *O*. Spring stop-screws *P* limit the extreme movements of the needle.

The method of using this instrument will be readily understood from the engravings. One form of test which may be made with it is that of investigating the uniformity of the lead of a supposedly accurate screw. In Fig. 32, for instance, the points are adjusted to span any suitable number of threads, and the instrument is pushed up to the screw to be measured until the measuring points are firmly pressed into the threads. Scale *M*, see Fig. 33, is then adjusted until the pointer indicates zero. The instrument is then moved from one place to another, along the thread, and in all positions the pointer should evidently indicate zero, if the thread is uniform in pitch through its entire length. If it is not uniform, this will be shown in the variation from zero in one direction or the other of the pointer on the dial; and the amount of variation can be read, since the dial is graduated to thousandths of an inch.

Another use of this tool is finding the amount by which threads are longer or shorter than the true pitch. In this kind of investigation the indicator is first set to zero, as previously described, on a model screw of known accuracy. The unknown screw to be tested is then put in place in the machine and measurements are taken at various points along its length. The readings given on the dial then show whether the pitch is long, short or irregular, and how much it is out in either case.

This instrument has the advantage of measuring on the sides of the thread at or near the pitch line. The indicating points are given the shape of balls, and various sizes are provided to suit various pitches and shapes of threads. An extra set is shown at Q in Fig. 32. Various model screws for comparative measurements are also shown in this

Fig. 34. Thread Testing Instrument with V-block Work-holders in Use

engraving at R, and bars of various lengths for carrying the fixed indicating point are shown at K_1 and K_2. The whole arrangement makes the instrument practically universal in application, since base-plates of any length may be used, or long lead-screws may be held on any plane surface, suitably supported with their center lines parallel with the base and at the right height for this instrument. The thread indicator described, as well as the eccentric grinding attachment, were designed by Mr. Epright of the Juniata shops.

CHAPTER III

MILLING CUTTER PRACTICE IN A RAILROAD SHOP*

In MACHINERY's Reference Book No. 79, "LOCOMOTIVE BUILDING, Part I. Main and Side Rods," the practice at the Juniata Shops of the Pennsylvania Railroad in making locomotive main and side rods, is described. Fig. 8 in that Reference Book, shows the operation of channeling the main rods on a heavy planer-type milling machine. The accompanying illustration, Fig. 35, shows a nearer view of the cutters and the work. The intermediate support for the arbor between the two cutters is here plainly shown. As was stated, the use of this support has materially increased the output of the machine, since it practically does away with the tendency to chatter, and with the consequent disintegrating effect on the cutting edges.

Fig. 35. Helical Blade Channel Milling Cutters, with Intermediate Arbor Support

The size of the arbor is also an important consideration. The hole in the cutters is made approximately one-half the cutter diameter. If the cutter diameter is, say, 8 or 8½ inches, the hole for the arbor is made 4 inches; or if it is 4½ inches, the arbor hole will be 2¼ inches, and so on. This practice has eliminated the troubles due to bent, twisted or broken arbors.

The principal point of interest in Fig. 35, however, is the construction of the cutters themselves. These, it will be seen, are of the inserted tooth type, with the blades held in place by screws and cylindrical bushings, the latter having flat tapered faces which wedge against the blades when the screws are tightened up. The novelty in

* MACHINERY, Railway Edition, October, 1910.

the construction of these cutters lies in the fact that the blades and the grooves in which they are set are formed to true helices, instead of being straight as is the usual practice. The importance of this construction has been pointed out in connection with the Taylor-Newbold inserted tooth milling cutter, described in a paper read some years ago by Messrs. Lewis and Taylor before the American Society of Mechanical Engineers. The use of the helical blade gives a constant cutting angle for the full width of the cutter. Otherwise, a variable cutting angle is obtained, which is too acute at one end, too obtuse at the other, and right only in the middle.

The method of cutting slots for receiving the helical blades is shown in Figs. 36 and 37. A Richards type shaper is used, as shown in

Fig. 36. Richards Type Shaper fitted with Attachment for Grooving Milling Cutter Bodies

Fig. 36, with the bridge piece inserted to make a continuous work-table. On this are mounted the head- and tail-stock centers, *A* and *B*, more clearly shown in Fig. 37. Between the centers is held an arbor *D* carrying at one end the cutter body *C* to be grooved, and at the other an index plate *E* provided with a number of notches, to correspond with the number of teeth the cutter is to have. On the hub of this index plate is loosely mounted a spur gear *F* which meshes with a short rack *G*, free to slide crossways of the axis of the work in the slots formed to receive it in the two uprights *H* as shown. A latch *J*, which is attached to gear *F*, may be engaged with any one of the notches in index plate *E*.

To the ways on which the tool carriage slides is attached the bracket *K*, on which is mounted the guide *L*. Block *M*, pivoted to rack *G*, is confined in the slot of guide *L* and is free to slide in it. *L* may be set to any desired angular position on *K*, through a wide adjustment, being provided with circular slots and adjusting bolts.

The operation of this fixture will be readily understood. As the tool carriage *N* is traversed back and forth on the cutting and return strokes, bracket *K* and guide *L*, being connected with it, are given the same motion. The inclination at which the slot in *L* is set, thus gives a back-and-forth cross motion to rack *G*, which in turn imparts a back-and-forth rotary motion to gear *F* and the work *C*. By setting the slot in *L* parallel with the ways in the tool carriage, no motion would be given to *G*, and a straight slot would be cut in *C*; the more the inclination given to guide *L*, the greater the angle of the helix cut in the work. After each slot has been cut, the tool is withdrawn, latch *J* is raised, and the work is indexed to a new position, latch *J* being dropped into the next notch. The next slot is then cut, and so on. This scheme works out somewhat better for the Richards type of shaper than it does for the standard machine shop design.

After the body of the milling cutter has had the slots planed in it, it is drilled and counterbored for the bushings which hold the blades

Fig. 37. Details of Helical Cutter Grooving Attatchment

in place. The method of drilling and counterboring the holes for these bushings is shown in Fig. 38. The same fixture is used as in Figs. 36 and 37, though the rack and the slotted yoke mechanism is discarded, and a bracket *P* is clamped to the base of the device as shown. This knee *P* is provided with ways on which may be adjusted the slide *Q*, carrying the drill bushing. *Q* is adjusted on *P* by hand-wheel *R* and the lead-screw to which it is connected. Besides carrying the bushing, slide *Q* is provided with a guide which fits the slots cut in the work in the previous operation.

The whole fixture, as thus arranged, is set up on the table of the drill press. Slide *Q* is then adjusted until its guide enters one of the slots and locates the work, with the bushings set at the proper distance from the edge for the first hole. This is drilled. Then *Q* is adjusted still further to the right to the proper position for the second hole, which is drilled; and then for the third hole in turn, and to still more, if there are more than three clamp bushings to each blade. Slide *Q* is then withdrawn to allow the guide to enter the next slot, when the operation is repeated, all the bushing holes being drilled in a similar manner. For the counterboring, the slide is set to bring the drill spindle into the proper position for a hole in the first row, the counterbore is put into place, the slide moved to one side, and the hole is counterbored to the proper depth. The work is rotated to the next hole in the same circle, which is also counterbored, and so on. The fixture is then set for the second and third rows of holes in turn. It will be seen that the fixture, when used in this way, locates each hole from the slot carrying the blade which is to be clamped by the bushing in that hole, and thus all the holes are accurately located.

The blades used are drop forged to true helical form, in dies whose shape is given them in the same fixture as that used in Figs. 36 and 37, for planing the grooves in the cutter bodies themselves. Assurance is thus given that the blades will be shaped to accurately fit in

Fig. 38. Jig for Drilling and Counterboring Holes in Cutter Body

the slots, leaving nothing more than a smoothing off of the scale to be done when fitting them into the bodies.

Another interesting point in the cutter practice of the Juniata Shops relates to the method of sharpening the inserted blades of rotary planer heads. They have experimented at the shop with various forms of grinding devices, including those in which the cutters are sharpened while in place in the heads of the machine. The main objection to this method of sharpening is that it ties up the machine while the blades are being ground. It was considered that this disadvantage more than offset the advantage of convenience, which this grinding attachment certainly possesses.

The standard practice now followed for rotary planer heads is to keep two sets of blades for each head, of which one set is in use in the machine, while the other set is being ground and held in reserve in the tool-room. All the blades of each set are ground at the same time, in a fixture which insures that the length over-all of all the blades in the set will be identical. The heads themselves (see **Fig. 39,**) are provided with abutments which locate the rear end of the blades, and thus give assurance that the cutting edges of all of them will project to exactly the same distance from the face of the head.

In Fig. 39, this abutment consists of a ring, supported on studs, as shown, and carefully located so as to have its inner face set at the same distance from the face of the cutter head all around. In Fig 40 is shown another head, which has a ring bolted to the back face,

Fig. 39. Rotary Planer Heads, with Abutment Ring for Locating Removable Blades

Fig. 40. Another Design of Cutter Head with Abutment Ring

closing the ends of the slots in which the blades are set. The blades are backed against this ring to give them the desired setting.

With the cutting edges accurately ground on all the blades, both with relation to the side of the blade on which they are clamped and the end of the blade by which they are located, assurance is given that they will all be set properly so that each will do its share of the work and leave a true surface.

MACHINERY'S REFERENCE SERIES

EACH NUMBER IS ONE UNIT IN A COMPLETE LIBRARY OF
MACHINE DESIGN AND SHOP PRACTICE REVISED AND
REPUBLISHED FROM MACHINERY

NUMBER 83

LOCOMOTIVE BUILDING

By Ralph E. Flanders

Second Edition

PART V

BOILER SHOP PRACTICE

CONTENTS

LOCOMOTIVE BUILDING

BOILER SHOP PRACTICE*

Boiler work has a distinctive character of its own, apart from the other machining operations of the locomotive plant. In fact, it is not composed so much of machining operations as of *tailoring* operations. It has all the characteristics of the tailor's art, though carried out on a much larger scale and with intractable materials. Sheets are carefully cut out to patterns, shaped in turn to suit either rounded or angular forms (both kinds are met with in tailoring). These sheets are riveted together instead of being sewed, but that is a mere matter of detail. This cutting and fitting requires experience, judgment and a certain special knack, if smoothly made and creditable work is

Fig. I. The Stock Yard of the Juniata Boiler Shop

desired. The more one sees of the boilermaker's work, the more credit one is inclined to give him for his ability to shape heavy sheet metal, especially in the case of so complicated and difficult a structure as the locomotive boiler.

In the first place, the locomotive boiler demands the highest skill of the boilermaker. There is more flanged work, more irregular bending of sheets, more difficult joints to make, than in any other type. Perhaps the Scotch marine boiler comes next in difficulty, but it is by no means a close second. An inspection of the consolidation locomotive boiler shown in Fig. 14, and of the various detail pieces shown in the other engravings, should carry conviction on this point.

*MACHINERY, Railway Edition, November, 1910.

Fig. 2. The Shop Crane run out over the Stock Yard, through Special Doors

This treatise explains in detail the separate operations for each step in the making of a locomotive boiler.

The Boiler Shop

The boiler shop of the Juniata locomotive building plant of the Pennsylvania R. R. is 722½ feet long by 80 feet wide. At the south end, as seen in Figs. 1 and 2, is located the stock yard in which the material to make up the boilers is stored. The regular crane runways of the building are carried out into this yard as shown, special openings in the end wall of the building being prepared to allow the passage of the crane. These openings are covered by swinging doors which may be let down from above; these doors are shown closed in Fig. 1 and open in Fig. 2. Inside the shop the machinery, furnaces, etc., are so arranged that the material passes from the stock yard through to the erecting and riveting floor at the lower end, and thence out into the locomotive erecting shop beyond, without backward moves except in a few unimportant instances. This flow of material is steady and regular, and it is seldom that any one of the three cranes is seen carrying a piece of work backwards for any distance.

Walking down the center aisle, the first thing met with on the left is the laying-out department, where the sheets are marked for trimming and punching. On the right is the lay-out table where flanged work is marked off for punching. Further down on the right and on the left are the punching machines, both for boiler sheets and for the tank work. A large automatic spacing punch is provided for the latter, which, on plain tank work, reduces the time of the punching operations almost to a negligible quantity, doing away with the laying out of the holes and the shifting of the sheets by hand.

Continuing further down we come to the drill presses and the bending rolls, and to the hydraulic flanging presses and furnaces on the left. A short space of the shop on the right is taken up by the tank work, and on the left by miscellaneous operations, such as flue cutting, welding, etc., and pipe bending. Next on both sides of the aisle comes the erecting and assembling space, with the riveting tower at the farther end.

In Fig. 14 is shown a drawing of the boiler of the H-8-B type of consolidation locomotive, illustrated and described in MACHINERY'S Reference Book No. 79, "Locomotive Building, Part I, Main and Side Rods." The important dimensions of this boiler are given, so as to convey an idea of the size of the work. It is probably the largest boiler ever made for consolidation locomotives. It is of the Belpaire type, as shown best in the firebox-end section. Instead of having radial crown stays in this type, the roof and crown sheets *O* and *L* are comparatively flat; the two are stayed together, while the upper edges of the side sheets *N* are stayed across to each other over the crown sheet.

One of the advantages of this type, from the standpoint of the experience of the Pennsylvania R. R., is that it allows the fire-box a better chance to "breathe"; that is to say, it gives it greater flexibility for

Fig. 3. Lay-out Floor, where Rivet Holes, etc., are transferred to the Sheets

taking care of the distortions that are inevitable when the heat of the fire and the pressure of the steam are applied. For this same purpose of obtaining greater flexibility, it will be noted that all the sheets of the rear end of the boiler are unusually thin. The fire-box and crown sheets, *K* and *L*, are ¾ inch, as is quite common. The side sheets *N* and the roof sheet *O*, however, are also only ¾ inch, which is uncommon. With this thin material, it is evident that the whole of the rear end of the boiler depends for its strength even more than usual upon the carefully laid out system of supports provided. But the whole construction gives to this part of the boiler a great flexibility, which it stands well in need of under the trying conditions to which it is subjected. To still further increase the flexibility, some of the more recent designs of boilers now have the back end sheet *P* stayed at the top from the rear barrel *E* of the boiler, next to the dome, instead of from the roof sheet *O*. This gives still greater freedom of movement.

Fig. 4. Transferring the Pattern on a Dome Course Sheet

Some other peculiarities of construction may be noted. One of them is the charcoal iron ring shown at *C*. This forms the connection between the slope sheet *D*, the front flue sheet *B*, and the smoke-box *A*, each of which is separately riveted to it instead of being riveted to each other. This design was adopted because it was found that considerable corrosion took place, for some reason, at this point on the bottom of the boiler; and pure iron is, of course, the most satisfactory boiler material for resisting chemical action.

Laying out, Punching and Trimming the Barrel Sheets

We will begin the description of the shop operations with those of the cylindrical or barrel sheets, as they are the simplest and most easily understood. At this shop the sheets are all received cut accurately to size by the makers at the mill, with a very small allowance for trimming. Piles of these cut sheets are shown in the view of the yard in Figs. 1 and 2. In looking over this material the writer found a sheet laid aside and chalk-marked with the legend "Do not use; no test piece found." Inquiry revealed the fact that every separate sheet used in every locomotive boiler on this road, has two test pieces cut from it at the mill by, or under the supervision of, the railroad company's inspector. These test pieces are numbered to correspond with the sheet, and are sent to the test plant at Altoona. Here they are subject to both physical and chemical tests, the results of which are recorded for future use. No sheets are used whose pedigree is not thus investigated and recorded.

The laying out department is shown in Figs. 3 and 4. A pile of sheets is laid on the horses as shown, and a templet is dropped on the top sheet by a crane. This templet consists of a piece of ⅜ inch (or thereabouts) boiler steel, carefully cut to the proper shape, and with all punched and drilled holes and openings accurately located and machined. The punched holes and the small drilled holes are all

Fig. 5. Punching the Rivet Holes in a Dome Course Sheet

marked through onto the sheet below by means of a prick-punch having a large body, fitting the hole in the pattern. The openings which are to be formed by punching out stock are marked through with a soap-stone pencil. The pattern is lifted out, the marked piece is taken away to be shaped and punched, and the pattern is replaced on the next piece of the pile, which is marked in turn.

A little wrinkle used by the lay-off men enables them to shift the sheets off the pile without the help of the crane, if necessary. By raising the sheet which is to be moved and placing large steel balls under it at different points, the sheet may be readily rolled off from the pile.

After being marked out, the sheets go to the punches. As shown in Fig. 5 these are of both the hydraulic and mechanically operated types. The punch itself is provided with a center point, which must be located in the center marked for each hole in the plate by the men who transferred the pattern. The sheet is hung from the crane so as to slightly over-balance, the edge under the punch being heaviest. The plate handler bears down on the outer edge of the sheet, bringing it up against the punch until he feels the point on the latter entering the center hole punched in the sheet. After the sheet is thus located, the operator presses the lever and the hole is punched.

The next operation on flat sheet work consists in drilling out the punched holes to the required size. Holes are punched 1/16 inch smaller for rivets up to ¾ inch, and ⅛ inch smaller for rivets above that size. The excess metal is then drilled out so that no incipient cracks or other harmful conditions will be left from the punching

Fig. 6. The Sheet Planer at Work on a Smoke Box Sheet

action. This has been found eminently satisfactory in practice, and avoids the more costly (though theoretically proper) operation of drilling the holes complete.

It should be noted particularly that it is the general practice here to punch and ream all the holes in all the sheets before sending them to the erecting department. The patterns are so carefully made and laid out, and the machine work is so accurately done, that the holes at the joints are expected to ream together throughout the whole structure, when the workmen come to build up the boiler out of the separate parts. The only exception to this rule is in the matter of those rivet holes which come on the scarfed edges of sheets where overlapped joints are made, such, for instance, as are found where the throat sheet *G* and neck piece *H* overlap under the side sheet *N* in Fig. 14. As a little extra hammering may have to be done here to make a good fit, it is not safe to punch the holes at the start-off. On the flanged parts also, as will be described later, special conditions are met with which require punching the holes at different times; but in practically all cases this is done before assembling. This practice results in great economy of time and labor over what would be possible if it were required to take the sheets back to be punched and reamed during the fitting operation. The drift pin is, of course, tabooed.

Besides being drilled and reamed, the edges of the sheet have to be trimmed accurately. This is done in the plate planer. For certain edges of no particular importance it is sufficient to leave them as they came from the steel mill. All edges that are to be calked, however, have their edges planed at the proper bevel so as to make a good joint; and the edges on the cylindrical sheets where butt joints are made are also planed to square edges in a similar fashion. The plate planing machine is shown in Fig. 6. This well-known machine is provided with a wide table, and carries a clamping bar having a number of

Fig. 7. Special Edge Bending Die in Place on the Rolls

jacks for holding the work in place. The reciprocating tool head carries a reversible holder, so that it cuts both ways. The feed is by hand.

Bending the Sheets

The sheets have next to be accurately rolled to the proper diameter. This is done in the power bending rolls, of which there are two different sizes provided, the largest being shown in Figs. 7 and 8. These rolls are driven by independent motors, with power vertical adjustment for the upper roll. This adjustment may be independently controlled for the two ends if desired, so that the roll may be tipped down at one end to roll conical shapes such as are required for slope sheet D in Fig. 14. The large roll is powerful enough to take care of inch-and-a-half metal, although it is not likely, of course, ever to be called upon to handle stock as heavy as this.

One of the difficulties of rolling heavy metal lies in carrying the curvature clear out to the very edges of the sheets, where they butt against each other. It has been customary to form the curves on these ends by hand hammering, or by dies under a special press. The operators of the rolls at the Juniata shops, however, have devised the simple scheme shown in Fig. 7 for accomplishing this in the rolls themselves. The die *R* is shoved in between the two lower rolls, by which it is supported. This die has a curved upper surface, concentric with the curvature of the upper roll. The flat sheet is supported by the crane and placed with one edge on this die, and then the upper roll is brought firmly down against it by power, bending it to the desired initial curvature. The sheet is next turned about and the other end is treated in the same fashion. The die is then removed, and the actual rolling commences.

The sheet is placed between the dies and the rolls, is carefully squared up, and is then passed back and forth between them from

Fig. 8. Rolling one of the Barrel Sheets

one end to the other while the upper roll is brought down closer and closer onto the sheet, giving a decreasing radius. The sheet is rolled to fit the curvature of a templet provided for the purpose, which is usually from two to three feet long. This is tried at various points around the circle to make sure that it will be of exactly the required curvature when the ends of the sheet finally meet in the completed circle. At points where the radius is larger than it ought to be, further passes through the roll will of course reduce it to the desired radius. Where, however, the radius, by some mishap is made too small, about the only possible remedy is to work it back again by hand hammering, and this occasionally has to be done, the sheet being held meanwhile in the rolls.

This matter of getting the sheet bent to an accurate circle is of great importance. If it is not bent to an accurate circle, not only will it not match well with the pieces to which it is riveted, but there is also danger of excessive strains in the boiler. When it is under pressure it tends naturally to take the circular shape, and if it was not in the circular shape in the first place, its struggle to arrive at that condition is sure to make trouble.

In sheets like the smoke-box and dome courses, where large openings have to be cut out for dome, whistle connection, stack, etc., the outlines of these openings are cut around on the punching machine leaving, however, the metal which is to be cut out still connected with the sheet by several "bridges" as shown at *S* in Fig. 4. The purpose of this is to make the bending as even as possible. In the case of the smoke-box sheet, for instance, were there no metal in the stack opening, the stock would bend so easily at that point that it would be given a sharp radius or corner. For this reason it is customary to wait until the sheets are bent before the openings are knocked out. Where, in bending, the edge of one of these pieces of excess metal projects and

Fig. 9. The 700-ton Hydraulic Flanging Press, and the Furnace
by which it is served

causes the plate to slip in the rolls, as sometimes happens, the plate can usually be started by throwing in a little sand between the roll and the plate to give the former a good grip.

The making of the slope sheet (*D* in Fig. 14) is similar to that of the smoke-box and dome courses except that it is rolled tapering. For this purpose the two bearings on the top roll are independently adjusted for height, so that a sheet can be bent to a smaller radius at one end than at the other.

The construction of the roll will be readily understood. The outboard bearing of the upper roll is arranged to be swung apart on either side to permit the finished rolled sheet to be drawn off over the end. The upper roll is meanwhile hung suspended and supported by a screw stirrup which anchors its rearward extension, shown in part at *T* in Fig. 8. The bending operation leaves the various smoke-box, dome course and slope sheets ready for building up into the finished boiler.

The Flanging Presses

In the early days of boiler-making flanging operations were avoided as far as possible. Where a sheet had to be flanged, it was heated locally in the forge and hammered to shape by hand. This was slow, costly and laborious; and it produced internal strains in the work. The locomotive boiler shown in Fig. 14 is pretty well covered with flanged work. This extensive use of irregularly bent sheets is only made possible by the modern hydraulic flanging press, whose use avoids all the disadvantages enumerated above as pertaining to hand work.

There are two presses for this work at the Juniata shops. The smaller of the two is shown in Figs. 11 and 12. It has six rams. The main ram, which supports the platen, is of 140 tons capacity. In addition, there are four adjustable cylinders and rams for holding-on, supporting die-rings, etc., which can exert a pressure of 20 tons each.

The large flanging press (one of the most powerful ever built) is shown by itself in Fig. 9, and in operation in Figs. 20, 21, 26, 27, and 31 to 36, inclusive. This machine has seven rams operating on the work, the arrangement being similar to that of the other press, except

Fig. 10. A Pile of Flanging Dies Stored in the Stock Yard

that there is an additional cylinder and ram on top of the upper platen, which is used for stripping work from the dies, and for forming the work in certain special cases. The main platen ram gives 700 tons pressure, the inner telescopic ram 200 tons, the four adjustable rams 28 tons each, and the upper ram on the top platen 100 tons.

Fig. 9 plainly shows at *U* two small, long stroke cylinders attached to the nearest corner of the upper platen, a similar pair of cylinders is mounted on the corner diagonally opposite. The pistons of these cylinders are attached by rods to the movable platen, and are used for adjusting it to position, ready for applying the pressure. The costly high-pressure water service is thus not wasted on the idle movements of the machine. The hydraulic pressure is generated and stored by a pump and accumulator in the central power house.

Internal strains, such as might possibly be generated in the flanging operations by the working of the metal, are avoided by a subsequent annealing. All flanged work is annealed the last thing before being removed from the flanging department. This is done by placing it in

the heating furnace, seen in the background of Fig. 9, raising it to an
even light red, and then removing it and laying it aside to cool in
some place sheltered from drafts of air.

A great point is made of having the machine flanging so accurate
that no local heating of any kind will be needed for hand flanging or
other operations. Local heating introduces strains which are difficult
to reckon with or remedy. Making the sheets as nearly right as
possible in the beginning thus results in better work, as well as in
work that is less expensive in the long run as a manufacturing proposition.

In Fig. 10, which shows a portion of the storage yard illustrated in
Figs. 1 and 2, is seen a pile of dies for the flanging work. Their
number (only a few of them are here seen) and their size will give
some indication of the importance of this work in modern locomotive
boiler construction. Specific information on the way in which these

Fig. 11. A Fire-door Sheet, and the Dies with which it is flanged

dies are used will be given in describing the making of each of the
different flanged parts.

The Back Head and Fire-door Sheets

These sheets, as shown at *P* and *M* in Fig. 14, and in Figs. 13
and 17 are flanged around the edges, and have the door opening
flanged in them as well. The blanks are laid off to templets or patterns, the same as for the various barrel sheets previously described.
Only the holes for rivets, staybolts, etc., in the face of the sheet are
marked, however, as it is evident that the stretching of the metal in
the flanging would make it impossible to locate the holes in the flanges.
These are left until later. A fire-door sheet all trimmed, punched and
reamed, and with the fire-door hole blanked out, is shown ready for
the press in Fig. 11. The dies are plainly shown in place on the small
press.

The operation is very simple. The dies are lined up and clamped in the press, the male die on the upper platen, and the female die on the lower or movable platen. Only the main plunger is used. In Fig. 12 the blank is shown lined up on the lower die, with the upper die just about to strike it and force it through, turning over the flange as required. A similar die, though on a much smaller scale, is used for

Fig. 12. The Fire-door Sheet in the Small Flanging Press

Fig. 13. The Fire-door Sheet on the Lay-out Table, for Locating the Holes in the Flanges

flanging the fire door opening. This is done in a separate head.

After the flanging, the sheet is taken to the lay-out table to have the rivet holes in the flange laid out. The sheet is set up at the proper angle so that the holes can be laid out directly from the vertical line on the drawing, and the locations are marked by surface gage, scale and scriber. This is shown in Fig. 13. For designs which are made

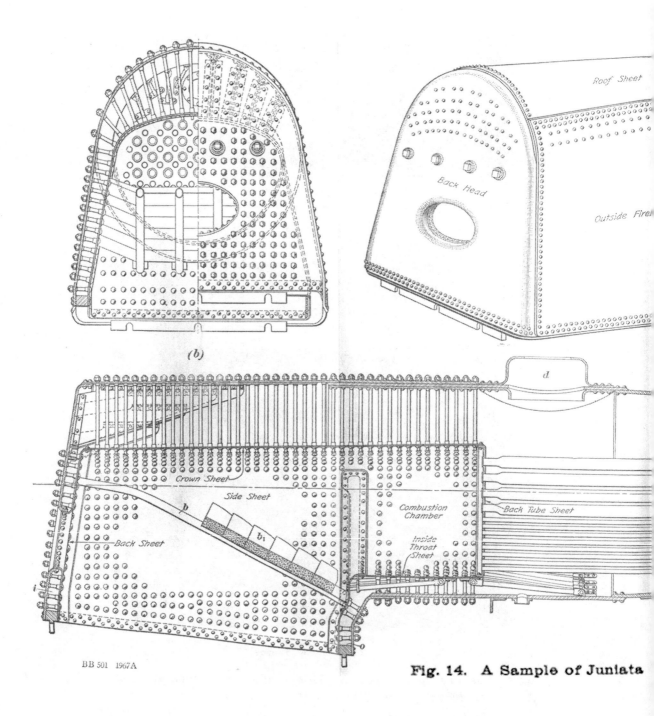

(b)

Roof Sheet

Back Head

Outside Fire

d

Crown Sheet

Side Sheet

b

b₁

Combustion Chamber

Back Tube Sheet

Inside Throat Sheet

Back Sheet

BB 501   1967A

Fig. 14.   A Sample of Juniata

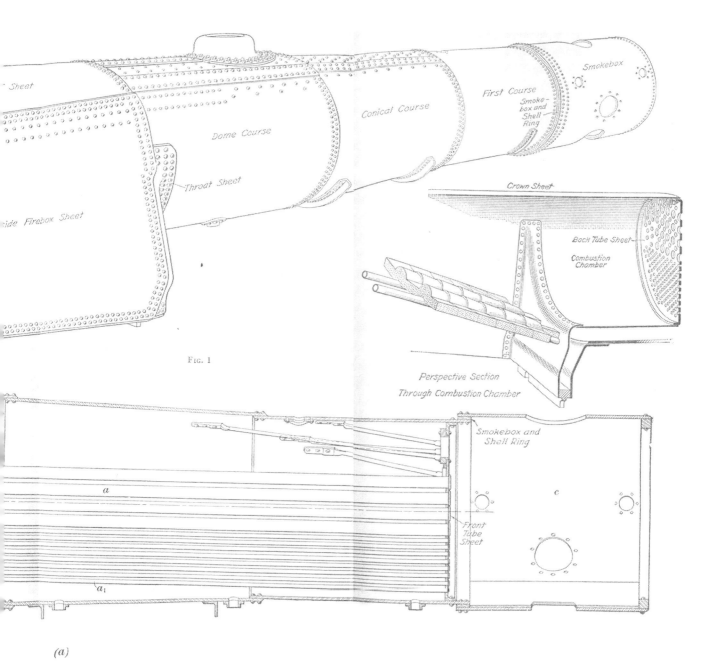

Sheet

Dome Course

Throat Sheet

side Firebox Sheet

Conical Course

First Course

Smokebox

Smoke-
box and
Shell
Ring

Crown Sheet

Back Tube Sheet

Combustion
Chamber

Fig. 1

Perspective Section
Through Combustion Chamber

a

a₁

Smokebox and
Shell Ring

c

Front
Tube
Sheet

(a)

ata Boiler   Heavy Consolidation Locomotive

in large quantities, templets are used for laying out these holes, as seen in Fig. 15. Here the surface gage is used simply for scribing a location for the templet.

Fig. 16 shows the methods and machine used for punching most of this flanged work. The riveter is of the horizontal, hydraulic type, to which the work is presented by a swinging crane. The sheet is suspended from it through a swivel hook, and may thus be easily turned to present any part of the flange to the riveter without readjustment of the support or of the work itself.

After the fire-door opening has been flanged, the rivet holes are punched in it by means of the hand screw hydraulic punch shown in Fig. 17. This is the only tool compact enough to work in the confined space which here has to be reckoned with. The punching of the corre-

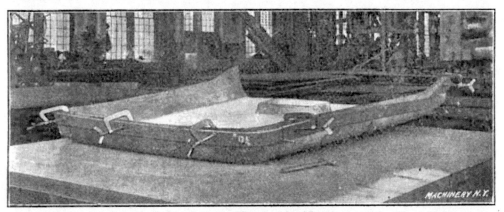

Fig. 15. Templets Clamped to the Flanges for Marking out the Rivet Holes

sponding holes in the inside fire door sheet is left until later, as this set of holes is one of the very few which has to be marked in place during the erecting, and punched afterwards.

The Flue and Throat Sheets

Both front and back flue-sheets, as shown in Figs. 14, 18 and 25, are flanged; the former is a plain circle, while the latter is bent to quite an irregular shape. As in the case of the fire-door and back sheets, the various flue, rivet and brace connection holes in the faces of the sheet are laid out with templets at the beginning, leaving the holes in the periphery to be laid out and punched after flanging. The operations in general are the same as in the preceding case.

The holes for the flue sheet are originally punched to a diameter of $1\frac{7}{8}$ inch for a 2-inch flue, leaving $\frac{1}{8}$ inch to be taken out in a counter-boring operation. This is the last machining operation, and is shown in Fig. 18. Fig. 25 shows a back flue-sheet with all the machine work completed.

One of the nicest pieces of work on the whole boiler is that of flanging and laying out the throat sheet. The blank for this is shown in Fig. 19. None of the holes are punched in this previous to flanging, as the whole sheet is of irregular form and is more or less drawn in the flanging operation. The dies are shown in place in the large press in Fig. 20. In the operation of flanging, the hot sheet is laid on top of the lower die, which is next raised up into contact with the upper die by the lifting cylinders *U* shown in Fig. 9.

The continued raising of the platen then bends the sheet down into the form between the upper and under dies, bringing it to the proper shape at one operation. The operation is shown completed in Fig. 21.

Fig. 16. Punching the Flange Rivet Holes in the Horizontal
Hydraulic Riveter

Fig. 17. Punching the Fire-door Flange Holes with the Hand-operated
Screw Punch

This job of flanging the throat sheet is one of the most particular in the lot, in the matter of getting the dies to the proper shape. To get some notion of the best way to form the dies in a new design, it is the custom at the Juniata shops to make model dies to a scale of say, ⅛ full size, and operate them in a hand press on a sheet of lead of the proper relative thickness. These miniature dies are made of hard wood, and are very carefully worked up by the die pattern maker, who works out the final full-sized pattern from which the actual steel dies are made. This man has to be a skilled workman, as the boiler designer does not usually lay out absolutely the full shape of the throat piece from every viewpoint. The case is, for instance, the same as if a ship builder should receive plan, longitudinal and end views of the hull of a vessel, and should then be required to determine the shape from this information.

Fig. 18. Counterboring the Flue Holes in the Front Flue Sheet

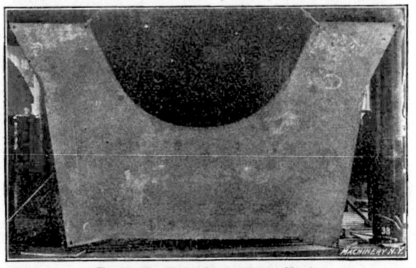

Fig. 19. The Blank for the Throat Sheet

One of the points he has to be careful about is to so shape the die that it will not draw the metal at points where the strength of the structure requires the full thickness of the original sheet. Questions of this kind are determined very readily by scribing off the surface of the model blank into regular squares. These lines will still appear on the finished model made in the wooden dies; and where the model has been drawn down, the squares will have been correspondingly distorted. It is thus possible to predict the exact behavior of the full-size dies in actual work, without risking the possibility of making them wrong in the first place, and producing spoiled work.

Tests were recently made with model dies and throat sheets for a new boiler in which the throat sheet is of unusual length and difficulty. It was found necessary in this case to tip the dies out of the

Fig. 20. The Throat Sheet Dies in the Big Flanging Press

Fig. 21. The Throat Sheet in the Dies at the Conclusion of the
Flanging Operation

horizontal plane, to prevent the sheet from creeping as the dies were brought together. The models revealed this necessity, which would otherwise have had to be learned at a considerable expense, after the manufacture of the parts was actually begun.

Fig. 22 shows the throat sheet after the flanging operation, set up on the lay-out table at the upper end of the room. This laying out of

the flanged parts accounts for the bulk of the cases where the work
has a backward movement; and this moving back is here justified by
the results. The man at the lay-out table sets the throat sheet up in
the same position as it will occupy in the boiler, and marks the position
of every hole (whether for stay-bolts, rivets, or other connections) over

Fig. 22. Throat Sheet on Lay-out Table, for Marking off Rivet
and Stay-bolt Holes, etc.

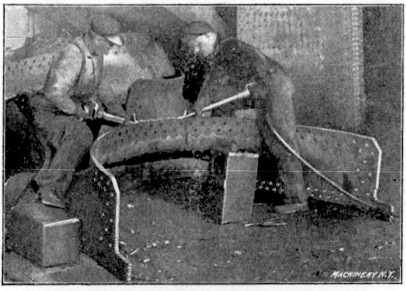

Fig. 23. Trimming the Edges of the Throat Sheet with the
Pneumatic Hammer

the whole sheet; the only holes not marked are the few rivet holes
which pass through the scarfed joint where the throat sheet and neck
piece come together. As previously explained, these holes are marked
and punched in place. The ability to lay out all these holes on the
table speaks volumes for the accuracy of machine flanging, and for

the accuracy, as well, of the numerous other operations which go to make up the various parts with which this throat sheet must match.

Irregular work like this cannot, of course, be trimmed in the plate planer, so the pneumatic hammer is resorted to, as shown in Fig. 23. Fig. 25 shows the completed throat sheet after it has been drilled and punched ready for assembling. It should be noted that many of the stay-bolt holes on the under side of the throat are drilled at a considerable angle with the face of the sheet. In such cases, instead of punching and then enlarging the hole with a drill as usual, the hole is first put through with a small drill, located by a center hole punched to a considerable depth; then the hole is machined out to the full diameter by a counterbore guided by a pilot fitting the preliminary

Fig. 24. The Blank for Making Two Neck Pieces

small hole, the same as for the tube sheet in Fig. 18. This prevents the slope of the throat sheet from forcing the hole away from the location given in the layout.

The neck piece, shown at H in Fig. 14, is characteristic of the Belpaire boiler. It occupies, on top of the boiler, a position corresponding to the throat sheet underneath, and has somewhat the same general form. It is naturally more difficult to flange, however. Nevertheless, this difficulty has been overcome by the exceedingly ingenious method adopted in this shop.

The illustrations Figs. 24, and 26 to 30 practically tell their own story. At the lay-out table the sheet is marked out for punching as shown in Fig. 24, the sheet being divided practically in two, as two finished parts are to be obtained from it. The space from V to W, and from X to Y is entirely open, while the rest of the blank is held in shape by bridges between the holes.

In Fig. 26 are shown the dies which, as may be seen, are direct in their action. The blank is placed in them, and is forced into the form by the ascent of the platen and lower die, as shown in Fig. 27. Figs. 28 and 29, showing interior and exterior views of the finished job of flanging, give away the secret. The difficulty lies, of course, in the forming of almost square corners at the top of the sheet without

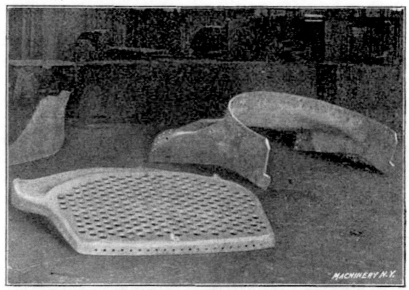

Fig. 25. Completed Throat Sheet and Back Flue Sheet

Fig. 26. The Dies for Flanging Two Neck Pieces at one Operation.

drawing out the metal to a dangerously thin section. By flanging two pieces at a time, with the holes punched as described, the metal is held together on each side everywhere, except at these corners. Here the blank has been cut entirely through, so that the metal is allowed to spread and draw into the corners, retaining practically its normal thickness over the whole extent of surface.

This ingenious flanging scheme likewise has the advantage of making a symmetrical job of drawing, so that there are no side strains on the dies, as is the case on the throat sheet, for instance, in Figs. 20

and 21. Altogether, these photographs are worthy of considerable study and thought on the part of readers interested in heavy flanging operations. They illustrate principles which should be useful in other difficult work. The double sheet, after being separated into its two

Fig. 27. The Flanging Dies at Work on the Neck Piece Sheet

Fig. 28. Interior View of the Neck Piece Sheet after Flanging

component parts, is taken to a lay-out table and is treated the same as the throat sheet, the finished work being shown in Fig. 30.

The Making of Solid Drawn Steam Domes

While considering this matter of flanging, it would be well to call attention to another unusual job, which is regularly performed in this shop. That is the drawing of steam domes from a flat sheet. This is illustrated in Figs. 31 to 37, Fig. 31 shows a blank and the first operation dies, in which the dome portion is drawn out. At Z is the telescoping plunger of the ram, fitted with a punch A rounded to the desired contour for the head of the dome. At *B* is the lower supporting ring of the die, mounted on the four clamping plungers *C*. At *D* is the upper ring die, clamped to the lower face of the top platen. The stripping plunger in the center of the upper platen is used for forcing the work out of the die at the conclusion of the stroke. *D* has a rounded corner on the inner edge of the die opening, so that the sheet will bend up into it smoothly, and with as little friction as possible.

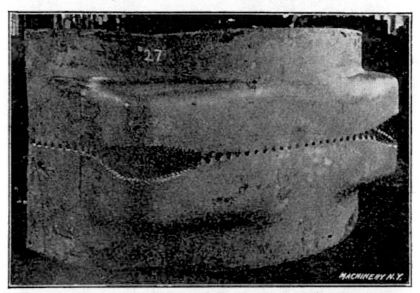

Fig. 29. Exterior View, showing Drawing away of Metal at Corners

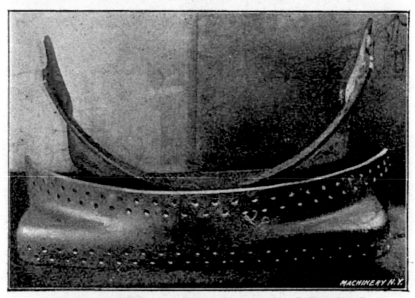

Fig. 30. The Two Neck Pieces Separated and Completed

Figs. 32 and 33 show the actual operation on the work. The great point is, of course, to avoid buckling and crinkling at the point where the flange joins the dome. This is avoided by the careful manipulation of the dies, and is done by bringing the upper and lower ring dies, *D* and *B*, just far enough apart at each successive operation, so that the metal is formed up into the dome shape by the plunger with-

out crinkling. This is a matter of judgment on the part of the operator. It usually takes about three heatings and press operations to
finally bring the dome to the condition indicated in Fig. 35 where it
is shown in place on the second operation or flanging dies.

The purpose of the second operation dies is, of course, to bend the
circular flange of the dome to fit the cylindrical sheet of the boiler.

Fig. 31. Circular Blank for Steam Dome in Place on Flanging Dies

Fig. 32. Steam Dome Blank after First Drawing Operation.

This is done in a single heat. Fig. 34 illustrates the dies. In Fig. 35
the blank is in place, ready for flanging, and in Fig. 36 the operation
is completed.

Sheet *E* has been placed over the lower die to enlarge the radius
of curvature given to the flange of the dome. By use of loose sheets
like this on both upper and lower dies, the same set of dies can be
used for domes for boilers of slightly varying diameter.

The finished dome, all punched, reamed and machined, with its various pop valve, whistle and throttle connections, is shown in Fig. 37. This particular dome is 31 inches in diameter by 15⅞ inches high above the top of the boiler. It is formed out of 1¼-inch steel. This is by no means the limit of drawing on work of this character,

Fig. 33. Blank after Second Drawing Operation

Fig. 34. The Dies for Forming the Flange

however, for domes have been successfully made in this way up to 30 inches in diameter and 24 inches in height, out of 1⅛-inch stock.

Miscellaneous Sheets and Other Parts

Fig. 39 shows the side sheet. This follows the same routine as the other plain sheets which have been decribed, about the only difference met with in its construction being the method of rolling it to the proper shape. As may be seen from Fig. 14, the back end of the regular Pennsylvania Belpaire fire box is out of square in every direction. It is narrower at the fire-door end than at the flue sheet. It is narrower at the top than at the bottom. It joins at the back end onto a straight sided fire-door sheet, while at the front end it is riveted to three sections, the upper one being the rectangular-shaped neck piece, the central section being the circular dome course of the barrel, while below it joins onto the flanges of the neck piece, which taper inward

Fig. 35. The Dome in Place on the Flanging Dies

Fig. 36. The Completed Dome ready for Removal from the Die

somewhat. This irregular contour at the front end has to blend into the straight section at the back end, evenly and gently over the whole surface—and this job of blending is up to the man with the bending rolls.

In work of this kind, there is comparatively little rolling to be done. The machine is used as a press instead, the power being applied by the heavy screws which adjust the height of the top roll. The oper-

ator shifts the sheets from one position to another in the rolls, bringing
the roll down with just the proper pressure to give the desired effect.
He has, of course, templets to go by in making the bends, but even with
templets the job is one that the amateur had better beware of. The
irregular shape of the sheet also affects the lay-out of the rivet and
stay-bolt holes in the templet. In the preliminary lay-out operation

Fig. 37. Steam Dome Machined, ready for Mounting on the Boiler

Fig. 38. Finishing the Foundation Ring on the Frame Slotter

on this sheet, the pattern has to be so made that the holes, as laid
out on the flat will come in the proper position after the sheet is bent
to the complicated form given to it.

The fire-box sheet shown in Fig. 40 is similar to the side sheet,
only it is not so difficult to make. The crown sheet, Fig. 41, is similar;
its shape is given to it by the bending rolls; it is accurately tested
by templets during the bending operation. Here, as may be seen, a

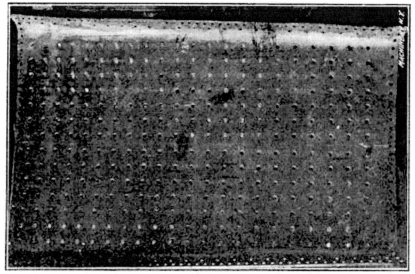

Fig. 41. The Completed Crown Sheet

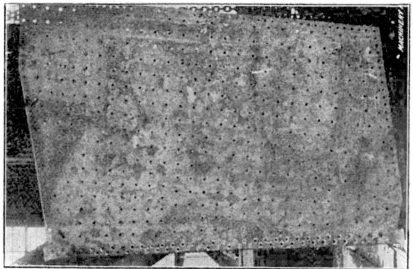

Fig. 40. The Completed Fire-box Sheet

Fig. 39. The Side Sheet Trimmed and Punched, ready for Flanging

bend of large radius is given over the top, while a small radius combined with straight edges, is used for the corners. The roof sheet shown in Fig. 42 requires the same handling.

Fig. 42. The Completed Roof Sheet

The foundation ring (or "mud ring" as it is perhaps more commonly called) is shown at Q in Fig. 14. This is a wrought-iron forging, finished accurately to dimensions, with its inner and outer peripheries machined all around. This machining includes the rounded inner and outer corners, which are finished to the proper shape so as to make a good fit when the time comes to rivet on the side, throat, fire box and other sheets. In Fig. 38 the foundation ring is shown mounted on the frame slotter, in the machine shop, having its corners fitted.

Other machine shop work is done on various boiler details. The front flue sheet, for instance, has its flanged edge trimmed and beveled to the proper angle for calking, by being mounted on the boring mill table, where it is accurately centered and turned. The charcoal iron ring (see C in Fig. 14) is similarly machined to accurate dimensions.

MACHINERY'S REFERENCE SERIES

EACH NUMBER IS ONE UNIT IN A COMPLETE LIBRARY OF
MACHINE DESIGN AND SHOP PRACTICE REVISED AND
REPUBLISHED FROM MACHINERY

NUMBER 84

LOCOMOTIVE BUILDING

By Ralph E. Flanders

PART VI

ERECTING PRACTICE

CONTENTS

LOCOMOTIVE BUILDING

ERECTING PRACTICE*

The Juniata Shops of the Pennsylvania Railroad at Altoona have a normal capacity for turning out a locomotive a day, the year round. Sometimes this capacity is exceeded. All the passenger locomotives used on the Pennsylvania lines, both east and west of Pittsburg, are built here, as well as many of the freight engines. There are but few other railroads in the country that make a regular business of building their own locomotives; and there are few other systems large enough to warrant such an undertaking, or to make possible a plant of the capacity of this one. It is large enough so that locomotives can be built in accordance with the best manufacturing practice for such work. In fact, conditions are perhaps a little better in this respect than in even the largest of the private plants, as the bulk of the work consists of comparatively few styles of locomotives.

We have described in previous parts of this review of locomotive manufacture (MACHINERY's Reference Series Nos. 79 to 83, inclusive), the detailed order of operations followed in manufacturing various important parts of the finished machine. It has been shown that accurate and rapid methods have been followed. The test of those methods, especially as regards accuracy, comes in the erecting department; for on the closeness with which the workmen follow the figures of the drawing, and on the fineness of their fitting, depend the rapidity and accuracy of the assembling. A study of the erecting methods at this plant serves to intensify the good impression gained from watching the detailed manufacturing operations.

The Organization of the Erecting Department

The erecting shop (see Fig. 2) is 579 feet, 9 inches long and 70 feet wide, and is served by four traveling cranes, two of 65 tons, and two of 35 tons capacity. The upper western end of the building is devoted to the wheel gang of twenty-eight men, whose work is described in MACHINERY's Reference Series No. 80, "Locomotive Building, Part II., Wheels, Axles and Driving Boxes." The middle section is used as storage space for boilers, frames, wheels, cylinder castings, etc., while the eastern end is used for the erecting proper—the south side being devoted to the frame gang, and the north to the actual setting up of the locomotive itself.

The work of erecting is divided between a number of gangs; these comprise the boiler-mounting gang of thirty-seven men, the frame gang of forty-eight men, the erecting gang of thirty-seven men, and the smaller sub-divisions, such as jacket gang, pipe gang, test gang, etc. These various bodies of men, whose work will now be described, are

*MACHINERY, Railway Edition, June, 1910.

Fig. 1. Parts Ready for the Frame Gang in the Assembling Shop

Fig. 2. Interior View of the Erecting Department in the Juniata Shops of the Pennsylvania Railroad at Altoona, Pa.

Fig. 3. A Frame Bolted and Fitted ready for Erection; Belpaire-Type Boiler in the Background

sufficient in number to turn out one machine a day under the favorable conditions which obtain here, both in manufacturing and erecting.

It is the business of the frame gang to set up the frames, and attach to them the saddle, cylinders, cross braces, foot plate, driver brake brackets, brake rigging, pilot, guides, crosshead, piston, etc. The material, as it is received by them, ready for assembling, is shown grouped together in Fig. 1. The particular parts here illustrated belong to a heavy consolidation-type freight locomotive of the H-8-B class,

Fig. 4. The Cylinders, Saddle, Frame, etc., ready for Erection

illustrated on page 4 and described on page 32 of MACHINERY's Reference Series No. 79, "Locomotive Building, Part I, Main and Side Rods." The section of the shop devoted to the frame gang is that at the left in the immediate foreground of the picture in Fig. 2, which space is there shown temporarily occupied by nearly completed locomotives.

The first job of the frame gang is the fitting and bolting together of the frame itself. This is, of course, made with one or more joints which have to be reamed and bolted together. The bolt holes for these joints come already drilled and counterbored. The two sections of the Atlantic-type frame in Fig. 3 have been blocked up until they are true with each other, as shown by measurement with a line and straightedge. When thus lined up, the holes in the joint are reamed with a pneumatic motor, the reamer having a taper of 3/32 inch per foot, the standard for this work. The operator, of course, has to take care that his reamer runs in just far enough so that the taper bolt, when driven up tightly to its head, will at the same time have a force-fit bearing along its whole length in the taper hole. To do this rapidly and accurately requires some skill, but it is soon acquired. In putting the frame together, the distance between the pedestal bearings is carefully measured, as shown later in Fig. 14. It is very important that the distance between wheel centers should be accurate.

Other work which has to be done on the frame at this time is the

Fig. 5. Frame Assembled with the Cross Bracing, etc.

fitting of the pedestal caps, equalizing bar supports, and similar parts. At the same time a man with a pneumatic hammer and specially shaped chisel has been going over the whole frame, rounding all the exposed corners. It is considered that this operation strengthens the frame somewhat, as fractures are more likely to start on sharp feather-edges than on smoothly rounded ones. After being thus fitted and finished, the frame is ready for assembling with its mate. It is then picked up by the crane and shifted to the point where the frame erection is to begin.

Setting Up the Frames

The frame is placed on blocking and jacks, an accurate spirit level being used to make sure that it is set horizontal. Next the foot plate is attached to it. Then the second frame is dropped into place beside the first and drawn firmly to its bearing against the foot plate, to which it is then clamped. The two frames are carefully checked up to see that they are level in themselves, and level with each other, straight-edges being laid across from one to the other for that purpose. Being found O. K. in this respect, the various cross braces, etc., are clamped in place, taper reamed and bolted, firmly tightening the whole structure together. This work of reaming and bolting continues throughout the whole of the frame erection, as the different subdivisions of the gang do not wait for each other; all pursue their own work simultaneously.

Fig. 6. The Assembled Cylinders Bolted to the Frame

Fig. 7. Testing Alignment of the Cylinder Flanges with the Pedestals

The consolidation-type locomotive, for which the parts in Fig. 1 are intended, is remarkable, as may be seen, for the weight and rigidity of the cross bracing. This serves the purpose of increasing the tractive power by its dead weight, as well as of strengthening the whole structure. Such rigid cross bracing was impossible with the Stephenson valve gear, which filled about all the space between the frames.

Fig. 8. Lining Up the Frame from the Cylinder Bore

The cylinders have next to be bolted in place. As shown in Fig. 4, the standard practice of the Pennsylvania Lines East is to use three-part cylinder castings, with the frame passing through a mortise in the joints between the saddle and the cylinders. This structure has the great advantage of permitting rapid and inexpensive replacement of cylinders in case of accident. It has been found practicable, for instance, to replace a cracked cylinder from stock and have the engine out on the road again, at work, within ten hours of the time of the accident. This would be impossible with a two-piece cylinder. The standard construction for the Pennsylvania Lines West, however, is a two-piece cylinder with the saddle split at the center line, and with the castings resting on top of the frames, instead of having the latter pass through them, as is the case in other designs frequently met with.

In any event, the cylinder casting and the forward extensions of the frame to which they are bolted, are assembled as a separate unit. The mortises and shoulders on the frame locate the castings, which are forced into place by wedge fits. If the machining is properly done, as it is expected to be in this shop, the cylinders, when bolted into place with the saddle and frames, will be parallel with each other, at the same height and the proper distance apart. When these parts have been assembled and found accurate in these dimensions, they are reamed and bolted together, and dropped into place in front of the frames, which are now in the condition shown in Fig. 5, ready to receive them. The crane lowers them into place, until bolts can

Fig. 9. Boiler and its Fittings ready for the Boiler-mounting Gang

be passed through two mating holes of the frame-splice on each side. The crane hook is then gently raised and lowered until the level shows that the castings are horizontal. The cylinders are then accurately adjusted and supported in this position by the jacks shown in Fig. 6.

Lining Up the Frames and Cylinders

Before finally reaming and bolting the splice in the frame (see Fig. 6) which holds the cylinders in place, the alignment of the whole structure as thus far built must be tested so that it may be jacked up and altered as may be required to bring the center lines of the cylinders into proper relation with each other and with the frame. The first step in this operation consists, as may be seen in Fig. 7, of testing the alignment of the cylinder flanges with the pedestals. A straightedge is passed through the two forward pedestals, resting on two supports of iron, to bring it to the proper height. A measuring bar is used, which is laid on this straightedge and brought up solidly against the face of the flange. The distance from the flange to the straightedge is marked. The same test is then made on the other side. If the measurements do not come the same, it will be necessary to correct the machining on the joint between the frame extension and the cylinders, so as to bring each side of the engine in line with the other.

Fig. 10. Smoke-box End with Steam Pipe in Place—Throttle, Nozzle, etc., ready for Mounting

The next lining-up operation consists in stretching lines through the bore of the cylinders, exactly on the center line, and testing the frame by them. This is shown in Fig. 8. The cord is supported at one end by a post mounted on a block of wood, which is anchored by any convenient weight—a heavy jack in this case. At the other end it is supported by a stick clamped in place by one of the flange bolts at the front end of the cylinder, and split to hold the pin to which the string is knotted. Both supports are adjusted up or down and to the right or left, as may be required to get them exactly on the center lines of the cylinder at each end. This is tested by a wire feeler or contact piece of a length slightly less than half the diameter of the cylinder. When one end of this touches the bore of the cylinder at any point, the other end must be just barely able to scrape the stretched line. With the line thus centered at each end of each cylinder bore, the erector proceeds to check up his frame.

In Fig. 8 a straightedge is shown laid across the two frames, ready to take measurements down to the line. This is done at various points along the length of the structure. Sidewise measurements are also taken between the line and the faces of the pedestal bearings, etc., to make sure that the frame is true sidewise. If it were out in any way, it would be sprung in one direction or the other, by jacks, into proper position, where it would be held while the rest of the erection proceeded. The clamping and bolting on of the various cross braces, etc., would then serve to hold it in this corrected shape. After all the parts shown in Fig. 1 have been assembled, the frame, which is now in the condition shown later in Fig. 13, is ready for the erecting gang.

The Boiler Mounting and Testing Gangs

While the work just described has been in progress, the boiler-mounting gang has been busy up toward the center of the shop. The raw materials with which they have to deal are shown in Fig. 9. Their work consists, as may be seen, in putting in the dry pipe, steam pipe, throttle, blow-off cock, and similar parts, shown scattered on the floor at the left of the engraving. Fig. 10 shows the smoke-box end with the steam pipe in place, and with the double-fulcrum type of throttle on the floor ready for mounting.

When the boiler has thus been provided with its main fittings, it is turned over into the hands of the man in charge of the boiler testing. It is located over a pit, as shown in Fig. 11, where connection is made with steam and water pipes, as may be required. The operation is a hydraulic test to a pressure of 256 pounds per square inch, the standard working pressure for the modern locomotives on the line being 205 pounds per square inch. After the satisfactory conclusion of this hydrostatic test, it is put under a steam test of 205 pounds, the two tests together lasting from 10 to 12 hours. The purpose of the steam test is, of course, to note the effect of the heat in conjunction with the pressure, and make sure that the expansion strains thus generated do not open any seams not affected by the cold test.

Insulation and Jacket Gangs

After the testing, the workmen in charge of the insulation and jacketing at once get to work. The magnesia lagging comes in sections which are applied and held on by wires, thin metal straps, etc. These

Fig. 11. Jacketing the Boiler

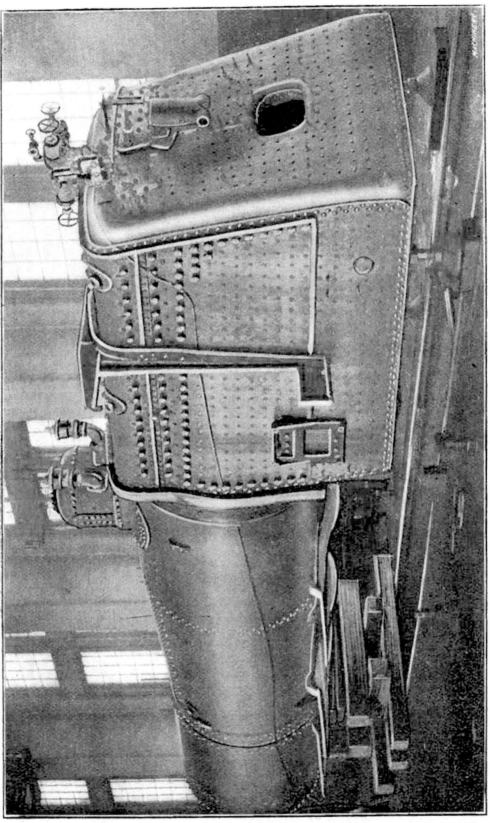

Fig. 12. Insulation in Place and Jackets Fitted

Fig. 13.   The Frames and Attached Parts as received by the Erecting Gang

are applied to cover the entire surface of the boiler, with the exception of the smoke box and lower portion of the fire box. The jacket gang then covers the whole with a soft steel jacket. On work of this kind experience and intelligence make a tremendous difference in the rate of progress. It is truly "fussy" work. These gangs begin immediately after the testing of the boiler, and continue their work practically through the rest of the erecting operations, up to the time the engine is run out of the shop. Evidences of their activity are to be seen in Figs. 11 and 12. The succeeding illustrations also show that they sometimes get a little ahead on their work, and sometimes fall a little behind. But it all has to come out even in the end.

The Work of the Erecting Gang

Meanwhile the frame with its attached parts, as set up by the frame gang, has been picked up by the crane and moved over onto the floor on the north side of the shop, and set down on jacks and trestles over the erecting pit, as shown in Fig. 13. The locomotive is supposed to be in the condition here illustrated when the erection gang receives it. Sometimes, however, the frame gang meets with delays, in which case the finishing touches are put on after the job is moved.

The first thing done in the new location is to again carefully level up the frame (the line is still in place in Fig. 15), and test its alignment in all directions with the cylinder bore. This is done both as a check on the previous work, and because mounting it on a new foundation invariably springs the structure to some extent. It will be seen that the trestles are of a special construction, which provides for both longitudinal and vertical adjustment. The use of these special trestles, in connection with the jacks, makes it very easy to bring the frame back into alignment if it is found to be out in any direction.

One of the next operations is that of marking off and fitting the shoes and wedges for the pedestal bearings. For this work the shoes and wedges are mounted in place as seen in Fig. 14, and firmly held there

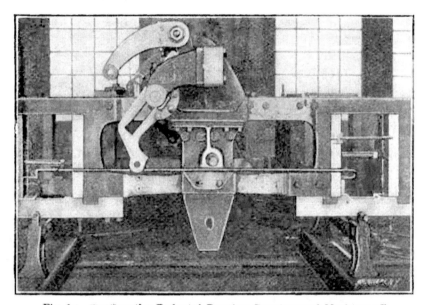

Fig. 14. Testing the Pedestal Bearing Spacing and Marking off
the Shoe and Wedge Fits

by the simple screw jacks shown. The shoe is left with a slight amount for finish, and it is the face of the shoe that has to be machined to give the desired fit for the driving boxes. For marking the amount to be removed, a scratch gage is employed, as shown; the block for this gage has a ledge, which guides it along the inner surface of the shoe while the scribing point is set to the required dimension from the face of the ledge; this marks the finish line on the shoe. The shoes are then taken to the planer and finished down to the line. This operation is necessary, because of the difficulty of getting the required closeness of fit by machining taper parts like the wedge and the tapered jaw of the pedestal to exact dimensions.

Fig. 14 also shows one of the inspecting operations performed by the erection gang. As shown, a fixed gage is being applied to test the distance between the faces of the shoes of two adjoining pedestals. This measurement must show accuracy to within the distance of one or two "pieces of paper" at the most—that is to say, within about 0.010 inch.

This accuracy is necessary, of course, both for the proper working of the side rods (which are bored to the same accuracy in length), and for the proper location of all the various parts of the valve mechanism. etc., the position of which is determined by measurements from the main bearings.

Fitting the Boiler

While this has been going on, another sub-division of the erecting gang has been fitting the boiler into place. In Fig 15 the boiler is shown dropped into place by the crane. It rests on the saddle at one end, and on the expansion pads at the rear end of the frame at the other. A chalk line has previously been drawn along the center line of the locomotive. This is leveled up by wedging the rear end of the boiler

Fig. 15. Trying the Boiler in Place for the Saddle Fit

to the proper height. The boiler is, of course, also centered on the frames. This is done at the rear end by taking measurements from the outside of the boiler at the fire box to the side of the frames on both sides At the front end the measurements are taken by a double plumb line, shown dimly in the engraving, hung over the front of the smoke box, from which measurements are also taken to the front ends of the frames. The boiler is wedged over one side or the other in the saddle fit to center it at the front, if this is necessary. At the same time the mud ring is tested with a level to make sure that the boiler is not placed out of the vertical at one side or the other. The boiler being thus accurately set, the flange of the saddle is heavily chalked, and a line is drawn with a scratch gage far enough away from the surface of the boiler to just finish out clear around the whole flange.

Note is taken of this measurement. If this finished line is ⅜ inch from the boiler, for instance, it is evident that the fire box will be ⅜ inch nearer the frames when the saddle is finished down to its bearing. The four expansion pads or bearings on which the boiler rests at the

Fig. 16. The Boiler Mounted on the Frame

fire box end, are therefore marked to finish out to a dimension ¾ inch less than that given by the position of the boiler in this trial setting. The holes for the side saddle bolts are also marked through onto the boiler at this time, after which it is again lifted off the frames.

Three or four men with pneumatic hammers now get to work on the job of bringing down the saddle to the proper bearing. Canvas curtains or screens are set up on the saddle, so that the chips made by one operator will not fly into the eyes of another. Many hands make light work on this job, so that by the time the bolt holes are drilled in the boiler and the expansion pads have been planed off to the proper height, this work of chipping and fitting is done.

The boiler is now permanently mounted in place on the frame, as shown in Fig. 16. The steel sheet which is bolted to the guide yoke and

Fig. 17. Lifting the Locomotive onto the Wheels

supports the boiler at the center is now marked off, drilled, and fitted into place. The bolting of the boiler to the saddle and to this central support, and the clamping in place of the expansion pads, now definitely lines up the frame and holds it firmly in the position in which it was set onto the trestles and jacks. The rigidity of the boiler is added to that of the frame, making a stiff, true structure of the whole.

While the operations just described have been going on, the crane has been bringing down the truck, drivers and trailer (if the locomotive is to have a trailer). The crane now picks up the boiler and its attached frame; the truck, drivers and trailer are rolled into place under it, and accurately located, and the engine is gently dropped onto its wheels. This operation is shown in Fig. 17.

Setting Up the Valve Motion

The locomotive is now ready for the assembling of the main and side rods, and of the valve gear. For this the machine work has all been done, the holes have all been drilled, and nothing remains save to put the parts in place and bolt them together. Absolute dependence is placed on the accuracy of the machining operations, and in the checking up of the frame and cylinder measurements as shown in Figs. 7, 8, and 14. Accuracy in the measurement of all the parts concerned is an absolute necessity for the proper building of locomotives with the Walschaerts valve gear, as this type of motion does not lend itself to the changes and corrections which are easily possible with the Stephenson link motion. As this accuracy, however, is a good thing in itself, in the way of shortening the time and expense of fitting and erection all along the line, it should be undertaken on any locomotive and with any type of valve gear. It is a paying practice from every standpoint.

Fig. 18. The Locomotive with Rods in Place ready for the Valve-setting Gang. Note Pile of Pipe in Foreground for the Pipe-fitting Gang

A locomotive with the valve gear assembled is shown in Fig. 18. About the only fitting which it is expected to find necessary, relates to the valve stem guide (see *T*. Fig. 20), which may have to be lined up a little to bring it accurately in line with the valve stem. There may also be an interference of the radius rod *R* with the valve-stem slide *O*, or with the yokes which support the pivots of the link *D*. Barring these interferences, which can be removed by a little chipping, the whole mechanism should go together with perfect freedom and with the proper amount of play.

Tramming for the Dead Centers

Valve setting with the Walschaerts gear is, as explained, a much simpler matter than with the Stephenson gear, since there is less leeway left for the workman in the way of adjustments. The first thing to do, as with any form of valve gear, is to locate the dead center points. This is done by the method shown in Fig. 19. First, the main driving axle is provided with an accurate center, as explained on page 27 of MACHINERY's Reference Series No. 80, "Locomotive Building, Part II,

Wheels, Axles and Driving Boxes." From this center an arc is struck
on the side of the tire as shown at *a-a*. For this work the driving wheel
has been mounted on the regular roller supports *X* operated by a ratchet
wrench and long lever, as shown also in Fig. 18.

The wheel is now turned until the cross-head is within a quarter
of an inch or so of the end of the stroke. Here, by means of a tram *g*,
a line is drawn on the side of the cross-head to mark the position. At
the same time by means of a longer tram *h* a line *b* is marked across
the arc on the tire of the driving wheel, the setting being taken from
any convenient point *f* on the frame or other stationary member. The
wheel is now turned past the center a little ways, and then reversed
and again moved toward the center. This is done to take up the backlash or play. When tram *g* shows that it is again at the same distance
from the end of its stroke as before, tram *h* is used to mark a new

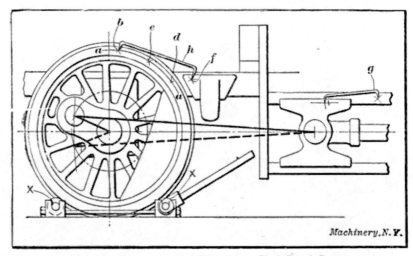

Fig. 19. Tramming the Wheels to Find Dead Center

line *d*, being set at the same point on the frame as before. With the
dividers, the distance between *b* and *d* on the tire is now halved, and
this point is marked at *e* with the prick-punch. The main driver is
again rotated by means of the roller mounting and ratchet wrench,
until the tram *h* lines up with points *e* and *f*, when the engine is evidently on the dead center. This operation is repeated at the other end
of the stroke, and also for the cylinder on the other side, so that
either side may be set to either dead center.

Marking the Admission Points

The Walschaerts gear for an Atlantic-type locomotive is shown in
two positions in Figs. 20 and 21. In the first case the piston *P* is at
mid-stroke, with the reserve lever and arm *G* set on the center. In the
second case the piston is at dead center, and the reverse lever is set
at the extreme end of the quadrant on the forward motion. The operator in charge of the valve setting has to check up the gear to make
sure that the lead is approximately constant for both valves at each end
of the valve for all positions of the reverse lever. He investigates this
by marking the lead on valve-rod cross-head *O*, as will now be explained.

He begins by scribing on valve-rod cross-head O the admission points of the valve—that is, the points at which the valve is just beginning to let steam into the cylinder. To do this, as shown in Fig. 22, the lead lever L and radius rod R have to be disconnected so that valve V can be moved back and forth freely. A horizontal line is then drawn on the face of valve-stem cross-head O with a scriber and rule. Each end of the valve chest is provided with inspection holes, as shown.

Fig. 22 shows the operation of finding the admission point at the left-hand port. Valve V is gently tapped into a position where the feeler shown, which is made of very thin metal, will just begin to enter between the edge of the port and the edge of the valve ring. This point can be seen by means of the lamp and mirror provided, which send the light down into the port. When this position has been found by feeling and sight, a tram, as shown, is set into a center point in a button permanently mounted on the valve chest end for the purpose, and a line is scribed across the horizontal line on the face of the valve-stem cross-head. The valve is now moved to the right, to the other end of the stroke, and the feeler, mirror and lamp are used in the same way to determine the admission point at the front end of the cylinder. This point is also scribed on the valve-stem cross-head in the same way.

The valve gear is now connected up again, and the engine is set on one of the dead center points, determined by the process previously shown in Fig. 19. This will bring the mechanism into the position shown in Fig. 21. The scriber is next applied in the same way as in Fig. 22, cutting a mark across the horizontal line on valve-stem cross-head O. Next, the reverse lever is thrown clear over and a second line scribed on O. Then the engine is returned to the opposite dead center, as indicated by the tire marks just made, and a third line scribed on O. Finally the reverse lever is thrown clear back, and a fourth line is scribed.

The Significance of the Valve Setting Marks

Now, if everything is all right, the lines thus drawn will appear as shown at Case No. 1 in Fig. 23. Here the two inner short cross lines were drawn by the method shown in Fig. 22, and show the points of admission, while the longer lines outside of them show the positions of the valve at the dead center points. The distance between the short and long lines on each side is evidently the amount of lead at each end of the stroke, which should be equal. Also, the lines drawn for the forward motion and for the backward motion should coincide, as shown, making one lead line, showing that the lead is equal for both full forward and full back motion.

It is more likely, however, that the marks will appear as in Case No. 2. That is, it will indicate more lead at one end of the stroke than at the other. If that is the case, it is necessary to lengthen or shorten the valve rod, as conditions may require, so as to equalize the lead at both ends of the stroke. The usual practice is to provide a threaded adjustment by means of which this change may be quickly made. The

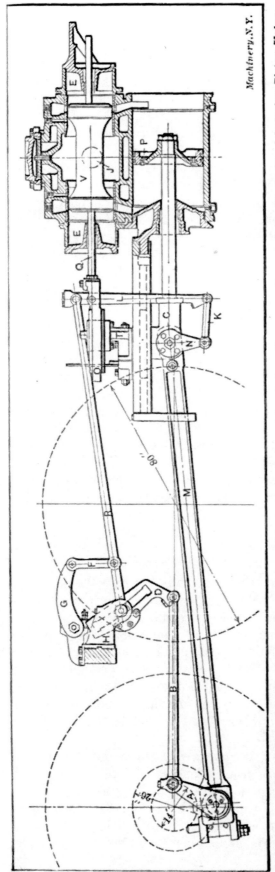

Machinery,N.Y.

Fig. 20. Section showing Cylinder and Walschaerts Valve Gear as used on Atlantic-type Passenger Locomotive with Inside Admission Piston Valve

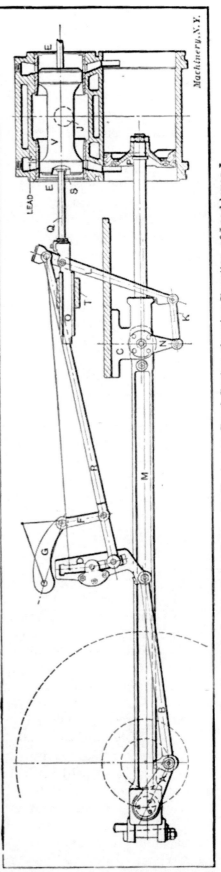

Machinery,N.Y.

Fig. 21. Walschaerts Valve Gear with Engine on Dead Center, showing Function of Lead-lever L

practice of the Pennsylvania road is to leave stock for fitting at shoulder S on the valve rod (see Fig. 21) and adjust the position of the valve on the rod by facing off this shoulder, or by putting in washers if that is required. The adjustment thus made is permanent. This policy is followed with the idea of setting the valve as it should be set, in the shop, and not leaving any leeway for changes by engine men on the road. It is thought best to take the matter of valve gear adjustment out of the hands of the engine men entirely, as it should be made right in the first place and should then stay right.

Now, in both Cases 1 and 2, the marks come the same for both forward and backward motion. This is as it should be, but they do not usually coincide exactly. For instance, Case 3 may be met with; here the lead is long for the forward motion and short for the backward at the front admission, and *vice versa* for the back admission. A little study of Fig. 21 will show the cause of this. Now in order to have the leads the same for both the forward motion and the backward motion, it is evident that, when the engine is on dead center as shown, it should be possible to swing the reverse lever from one end of the quadrant to the other without changing the lead; and to make this possible it is evident that the arc-shaped slot in link D, when the engine is thus set, must be accurately struck from the center of the pivot by which radius rod R is connected with lead lever L.

Now, in erecting the locomotive, if bracket H (see Fig. 20). which supports link D, is set too far forward or too far back, it is evident that link D will be tipped forward or back to correspond, throwing the center of its slot below or above the proper point at the pivot of the radius rod. Then the operation of the reverse lever will move the valve, giving a variable lead. If this mistake in the location of the links supporting the bracket has been made, about the only way out of the difficulty is to lengthen or shorten the return crank rod B, so as to again tip the link back to its proper neutral position. A study of the diagrams for Cases 3 and 4, in connection with Fig. 21, will show why the rod should be lengthened for one case and shortened for the other.

Now it is possible that, instead of having the marks come as in Cases 3 and 4, they will come as in Cases 5 and 6. That is, the lead will be too great at both ends of the forward motion, and too small at both ends of the backward motion, or *vice versa.* In a case of this sort it is evident that something else is at fault besides the position of link bracked H, or the length of return crank rod B. A difficulty of this kind is almost certain to be caused by the wrong location of return crank A on the crank-pin. In fastening it in place it is either swung too far forward or too far backward, as the case may be. If it is swung too far forward it is evident from Fig. 21 that the lead will be reduced on the forward motion at each end of the stroke, the gear being there shown in the forward position. If the reverse lever is thrown over and the radius rod R lifted to the upper end of link D for the backward motion, it is evident that, since we are on the other side of the center of the link, the lead will be increased at each end. This gives us Case 6. This can only be remedied by re-locating return crank *A* in the proper position, which must evidently be done by swinging it backward as much as may be required. An adjustment in the opposite direction must, of course, be taken for Case 5.

An examination of Figs. 20 and 21 shows plainly that the action of lead lever *L*, through its connection by link *K* and bracket *N* with cross-head *C*, must be relied upon entirely for obtaining the lead. The difficulties shown in Cases 3, 4, 5 and 6 arise from the fact that the connections through the return crank *A* and rod *B* are allowed to influence the lead, when they should not. In the position shown in Fig. 20 with the reverse lever on the center, the action of the return crank is entirely cut out; here the motion of the cross-head *C* will evidently give the normal lead to the valve. With the engine on dead center as shown in Fig. 21, swinging the reverse lever through the whole of its throw, and raising radius rod *R* from bottom to top of the link, should not move the valve, since the center of the slot should be con-

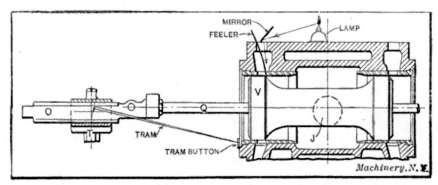

Fig. 22. **Marking the Admission Points on the Valve-rod Cross-head**

centric with the pivot between *R* and *L*. It should, in fact, allow the same lead as for Fig. 20. All the difficulties met with come from the fact that, either owing to the improper position of bracket *H* or of return crank *A*, the link is not so set that radius rod *R* can be thrown from one end to the other without altering the lead.

It is expected, of course, that before all the separate parts making up the valve motion come to the erecting shop, they shall have been inspected and found to be true to dimensions. It is also expected that the valve gear shall have been properly designed in the first place. With these two conditions looked out for, as they invariably are, the erecting shop's responsibility lies in the position of return crank *A* and the location of bracket *H*, and in getting the proper length of valve rod *L*. It is expected that the erecting gang will work close enough so that Cases 3, 4, 5 and 6 shall not appear in any engine bad enough to require alterations to be made. If changes of this kind are necessary, the case is one which requires investigation on the part of the foreman to locate the workman who has been at fault.

The diagram in Fig. 23 is correct for the right-hand side of the locomotive, with a piston valve giving inside admission. For the left-hand side, the diagram should be reversed, as though it were seen in a mirror. After studying the drawings the student will be able to make his own diagrams for engines having outside admission—a condition sometimes met with in practice where the Walschaerts gear has been applied to a slide valve.

The six cases shown will seldom be found in the unmixed form; the valve setter is more likely to find a mixture of Cases 3 and 5, for in-

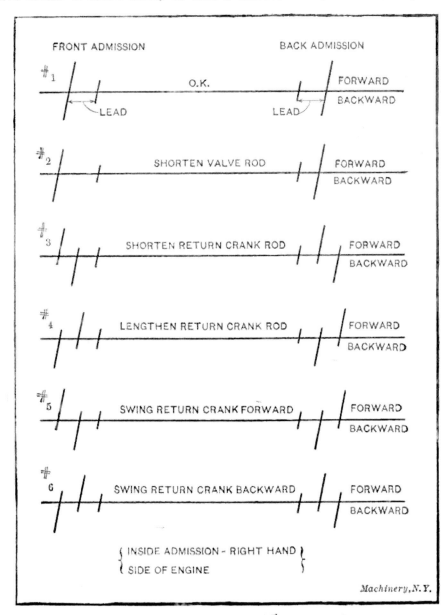

Fig. 23. Diagram showing Significance of Variations in Lead, as given by Admission and Dead Center Lines on the Valve-rod Cross-head

stance, or of Cases 2, 3 and 6. Where these mixed errors are serious, he should adjust one factor at a time, beginning with the correction of the length of the valve rod. At the Juniata shops a permanent record is kept of the amount of lead at each end of the stroke on both sides of each engine turned out. This is done for a number of positions of the reverse lever, from the neutral position to full motion in each direction. These reports are marked with the valve setter's name, and are kept for reference in case of complaint as to the running of the locomotive in service.

Miscellaneous Finishing Operations

Subdivisions of the erecting gang have been at work on various parts of the machine while the special operations described in the previous paragraphs have been in progress. The stack has been put in place, the bell has been mounted, the cab has been fitted, the brakes have been connected up, and the air pump mounted. The jacket gang has finished the fitting of the jacketing on the boiler and also on the cylinders and valve chest. The men on these various gangs have been swarming all over the locomotive together, and it requires a real "team spirit" for them to work effectively and still keep out of each other's way. Good work in erecting under conditions of this kind requires the maintenance of the proper feeling of the men toward each other, and toward the job on which they are engaged. If they do not have this feeling, the time required will be double that in which it ought to be done, or even longer.

One of the gangs whose work should be mentioned in particular, is the pipe gang. These men are a sub-division of the boiler-shop force, not being directly under the control of the erecting shop foreman. An interesting feature of their work is the fact that all the piping used about the locomotive is cut to length and bent to shape before being brought to the locomotive. This means that good work is done, not only in building the boiler correctly to the drawing, but also in locating the various connection holes, and in the actual work of cutting and bending the pipe. The resulting arrangement of piping work at the boiler end in the cab is very pleasing indeed, in its general appearance. This is shown in Fig. 24. The picture was a difficult one to get, owing to the abundance of black paint and shadows, but it illustrates the high character of the work done. On the floor in front of Fig. 18 is shown a pile of cut, bent and threaded pipes as they come from the boiler shop, ready for piping.   !

Another point of interest that may be mentioned is the method of locating the gage cocks. Their function, of course, is to determine the depth of the water over the crown sheet. The holes for these cocks might be located by measurements from the drawings, but to be on the safe side it is the practice here to actually take the measurements from the crown sheet itself. This is done in two ways, which are used to check up each other. A straightedge, carefully leveled up, is run in through the fire door, and a measurement is made from that to the crown sheet on the inside. A line is then drawn on the face of the boiler at the same height on the outside. This is used as the datum line for locating the gage cocks.

To check up this datum line, a hydrostatic device is used. A rubber tube is carried into the fire box, with its end held up against the under side of the crown sheet. A glass tube is inserted in its outer end at about the level of the crown sheet, and water is poured in until it commences to run out on the inside from the open end. The height of the water in the glass tube then locates the height of the end of the pipe on the inside, and thus the height of the crown sheet.

Results in Erection Work

It may be interesting to give some figures as to the number of men in the various gangs required for the normal output of one locomotive

Fig. 24. View into Cab of Locomotive, showing Neat Arrangement of the Piping, Valves, Injector, etc.

per day, and also to give some notion of the length of time required for the various processes of erection. The frame gang is composed of 48 men, and it spends about 27 working hours on the frame of a heavy locomotive. Not all of them, of course, are working on the same frame at the same time, but each engine is in the hands of the frame gang for the length of time indicated. The boiler-mounting gang com-

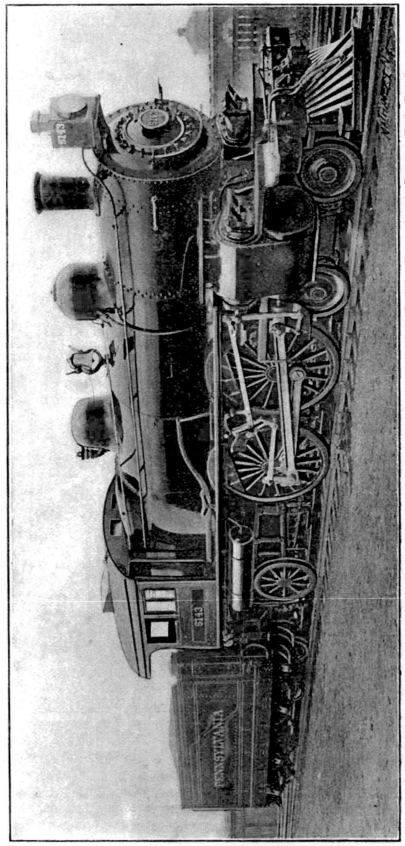

Fig. 25. Completed Passenger Locomotive of the Standard Atlantic Type, used on Regular Pennsylvania Express Train Service

prises 37 men, and the boiler stays in their hands for about 29 hours. The erecting gang is composed of 37 men, and the locomtive is in their hands for about 33 hours. The work of all these gangs overlaps, as explained; and there are besides these the miscelleaneous workmen such as the sheet-iron workers, pipe fitters, painters, etc. The quick work which these figures indicate is only made possible by accuracy in the machine shop operations, and by good organization on the part of the erecting force.

The rate of erection appears, to a person not acquainted with locomotive building practice, to be of almost bewildering rapidity. The machine-tool machinist is likely to think of a locomtive as being built rather slowly, something like a house. The writer had still some remnants of this idea left on his first visit to the shop. He had watched for a few hours the progress of a locomotive which was approaching completion. At the suggestion of the erection foreman he had climbed up into the cab, to examine the piping arrangements and other features to be seen there. What was his amazement, after a few minutes' conversation, to be approached by one of the workmen with an invitation to vacate, as he desired to run the engine out into the yard. The writer then realized for the first time that they had been getting up steam meanwhile from a stationary boiler, and that a touch on the reverse lever and the throttle was all that the big engine needed to get itself under way. The last finishing touches of the painters were put on as the locomotive rolled out into the yard.

That same evening, the writer saw the new machine going by, pushing away at the back end of a long freight-train which was starting on its twelve-mile struggle up the grade to the summit tunnel at Gallitzin. The long preliminary "workouts" which used to be considered necessary are not the regular practice here. The locomotive is expected to be built well enough to go into pusher service, at least, directly from the start. Practically all of them are subjected to this severe test.

It may be interesting to know that in the case of the consolidation locomotive which is illustrated in some of the photographs here used, 23,734 separate pieces in all are required for the whole machine. The number is probably somewhat less for the standard Atlantic-type locomotive from which the other illustrations were taken. This latter engine is shown complete, ready for the road, in Fig. 25.

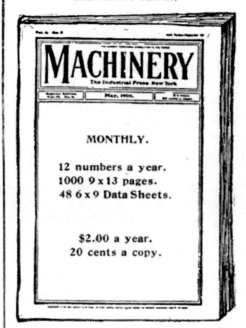
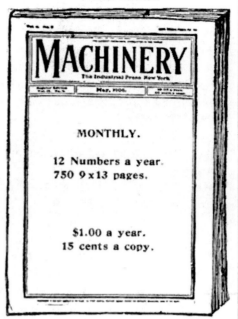

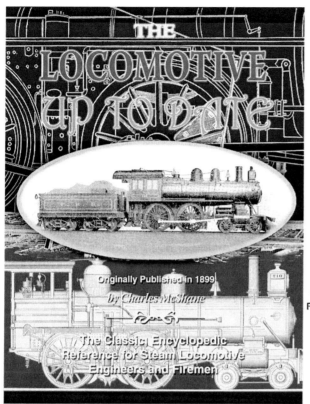
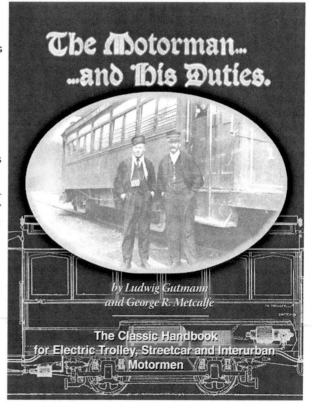

LaVergne, TN USA
03 December 2010
207336LV00003B/227/P